The Book of
Derby

The Book of
Derby

by
Anton Rippon

The Breedon Books
Publishing Company
Derby

First published in Great Britain by
The Breedon Books Publishing Company Limited
44 Friar Gate, Derby DE1 1DA
1993

Front cover shows: (right) Derby City Council photograph of Henry
Duesbury's 1841 Guildhall, floodlit in the late 1980s; (top left) St
Werburgh's Church from a nineteenth-century painting; (bottom left) the
Plumber's Arms in Bag Lane (now East Street) awaiting demolition in the
late 1870s. *Back cover shows:* Queen Street before World War Two,
picturing the Bull's Head, the Dolphin and the Silk Mill pubs.

Most of the photographs in this book are from the Derby Local Studies
Library Collection. Others are from several private collections and the
author gratefully acknowledges the use of all.

ISBN 1 873626 08 8

Printed and bound by Hillman Printers (Frome) Ltd.
Covers printed by BDC Printing Services Ltd of Derby.

Contents

Introduction

ALTHOUGH Derby cannot claim to be an historic city in the same way as York or Chester, it is, nevertheless, a city full of history. From the time the Romans made their camp at Derventio, through the Saxon village of Northworthy, to Derby's emergence as a Danish burgh, its stature has grown steadily.

Derby's story runs parallel with the history of England and it has shared in all the nation's great upheavals, political and social, civil and military.

The eighteenth century brought a handful of visionaries — John Lombe, William Duesbury, Jedidiah Strutt to name three — who would set Derby on a new path towards prosperity. The town was well prepared for the Industrial Revolution and the coming of the railways.

My own interest in Derby's story began as a small boy, wandering the rooms of Derby Museum and willing the Roman pottery and Saxon coins to give up their secrets. Or standing by the Derwent in Darley Fields and trying to imagine the scenes which must have met the legionary who first settled here. It was my late father who fired this interest. Although not a Derby man, he had lived here, with a short break, since 1932 and had come to love the town. He was certainly always ready to explore its history and he passed his interest on to me.

Alas, Derby does not have a good record of preserving its heritage and most of the old town has disappeared under the bulldozer — much of it quite needlessly. But it is still possible to trace the city's growth and whilst this is certainly not intended as a guide book, if it stimulates the reader to take a stroll in search of history, then so much the better.

The first edition of this work was published in 1980 and quickly sold out. Alas, the original publishers believed in modest print runs and the book has been unavailable for over a decade. This edition, published by my own company, has been updated where necessary and also includes some photographs which were not in the original edition.

Since 1980, of course, many further changes have occurred in Derby, not least the development of a tourist industry. For too long the city has been guilty of failing to promote itself but all that is now changing, for Derby is, as we have said, a town full of history as well as being a splendid base to explore further afield.

This book contains only a small amount of the material which I amassed in researching the city's past, but enough to tell the story of Derby. I set out to answer the questions I have always asked. What follows is my version of Derby's story, from earliest times to the present day.

A Poet's View

But when proud Derby's glittering vanes you view,
And her gay meads your sparkling currents drink;
Should Bright Eliza press the Morning Dew,
And bend her graceful footsteps to your brink,

Stop, gentle wave, in circling Eddies play,
And, as your scaly squadrons gaze around,
Quick let your Nymphs with Pencil fine pourtray
Her Angel Footsteps on your painted ground.

From *Ode to the River Derwent*
by Erasmus Darwin

Acknowledgements

In researching this book I made use of the many excellent publications on various aspects of Derby's story. I record my thanks to, and my admiration for, the authors of these publications for their painstaking spadework.

Thanks are also due to the Derbyshire County Library Service for the use of most of the photographs herein and to Derby City Council for the splendid photograph of the Guildhall used on the cover; to Mrs Ann Mellors, who was then in charge of Derby Local Studies Library, and to her successor, Sylvia Bown, and the admirable staff there; to R.G.Hughes, former principal keeper at Derby Museum; to former Councillor Jeffery Tillett and Bob Randall, former Editor-in-Chief of the *Derby Evening Telegraph*; to Peter Newton, Ron Frost and David Hannah who each helped in a variety of ways, not least with massive injections of enthusiasm; my wife Pat read the proofs of the original book and Dianne Davies and Pip Southall did that work on this new edition. My parents and my daughter also weighed in with their interest and support. Like most things to come out of Derby, this book is a team effort.

The Crossing of the Ways

WHY Derby? The very first question in tracing the story of an industrial city of some 217,000 souls, is simply to ask why it should be here in the first place.

The answer, as always, is purely geographical. Derby is at a point where the lowlands of the Midland Plain run up against the highlands of the Pennine Hills. To cross from east to west without tackling the hills, the traveller must pass close to Derby. If he wants to go north into the highlands of Britain, the River Derwent, which runs through the city, has cut a convenient path through the rocks; and the journey south over the plain is an easy and straightforward one. We are quite naturally, as W.Alfred Richardson said in his *Citizen's Derby*, at a crossing of the ways.

In addition to being splendidly placed for communications, Derby has always had the bonus of being within easy reach of a whole range of important rocks and minerals. The warm, clear sea which once covered Derbyshire eventually receded to leave behind its beds of coal, iron, lead, gypsum and clay. From the moment the land took shape, it was almost inevitable that Derby would be born.

Derbyshire's rocks are of two distinct ages and the Derby area sits on the younger Bunter Pebble Beds, Sandstones and Keuper Marls of the Triassic Age of 248 million years ago. The Keuper Marl of Derby is red mudstone which contains calcite, the substance formed in inland seas. There is also a superficial layer of Boulder Clays, Lacustrine Clays, sands and gravels of the latter Pleistocene or Ice Age.

Farm wall at Little Chester reputed to be made from stones from the Roman fort. Pictured c.1912.

Even today, the Derwent deposits alluvium. The Boulder Clays were formed by melting glaciers and the Lacustrine Clays, which are found in the south of the city, by lakes, in turn fed by rivers from those melting glaciers. The rivers themselves formed the sand and gravels and they are found in just one area, under Burton Road, to the west of the Arboretum, where they have caused several landslips in recent years.

Who, then, were the first people to settle and build dwellings in the area which is present-day Derby? Certainly not the Ancient Briton. Occasional discoveries of flints and axes suggest that hunters may have passed this way, but the farmer of Pre-Roman Britain would have found it almost impossible to pasture animals and cultivate crops in such a heavily-wooded lowland, for Derby was then a forest of oak and elm, and to a lesser extent, birch, lime and ash. The site of the city was then inhabited by brown bears, wolves, wild pigs and oxen, red deer, pine marten and polecat. There would have been no grey squirrels, cats or rats, for they were introduced by man much later.

It was the Romans who first lived here. They came about AD48 on their way to subdue the Brigantes, a British tribe which ruled the north, including Derbyshire. In building a line of forts beyond the Fosse Way, the Romans sought to establish the first boundary of their newly-conquered province. The forts stretched from Lincoln in the east to Ilchester in the south-west, and one of them was built on high ground overlooking the River Derwent. Thus, the first human settlement of Derby was sited around Belper Road. Roman military strategists soon realised the importance of the area and in AD80, they moved across the Derwent and built a new fort on the east bank, calling it Derventio.

The earliest Derventio — the Saxons later called it Little Chester and we still know it as that — was a wooden structure, but eventually, it was replaced by a more permanent stone encampment. Gradually, a civil settlement grew up around the camp and in the 1970s, an industrial suburb of Derventio was discovered on Derby Race-course, between Stores Road and Mansfield

Coin struck by Viking king in Northumbria and dated to the early tenth century. It was excavated at St Alkmund's Church.

Road. It had a road 25ft wide, lined with timber buildings, two pottery kilns and a cemetery, and would have lain half a mile to the east of Derventio on the old road to Sawley.

The great Roman Road of Rykneld Street, which connected the military garrisons of the wild north with the civilised Roman towns of the south, passed straight through the middle of Derventio, following the line of the present Nuns Street and crossing the Derwent near the old railway bridge. Rykneld Street left the camp to climb up the valley towards Chesterfield and along it must have marched Roman troops on their way to quell British resistance. A road taking the soldiers from east to west passed close to the foothills of the Pennines, and another vital highway followed the Derwent up into the lead mines of the Wirksworth area. To the north-west, a road led to the Roman bathing spa of

Buxton. For local bathing, incidentally, the Romans had their own baths on the banks of the Derwent at Parker's Piece where the playing fields of Derby School were later sited.

The Roman soldiers who lived in Derven-tio were most likely auxiliaries — colonial troops — and may have come from Gaul (modern-day France). Their prime tasks were to guard the junction of the highways, particularly the road to the lead mines, and to keep the Britons of the north Derbyshire

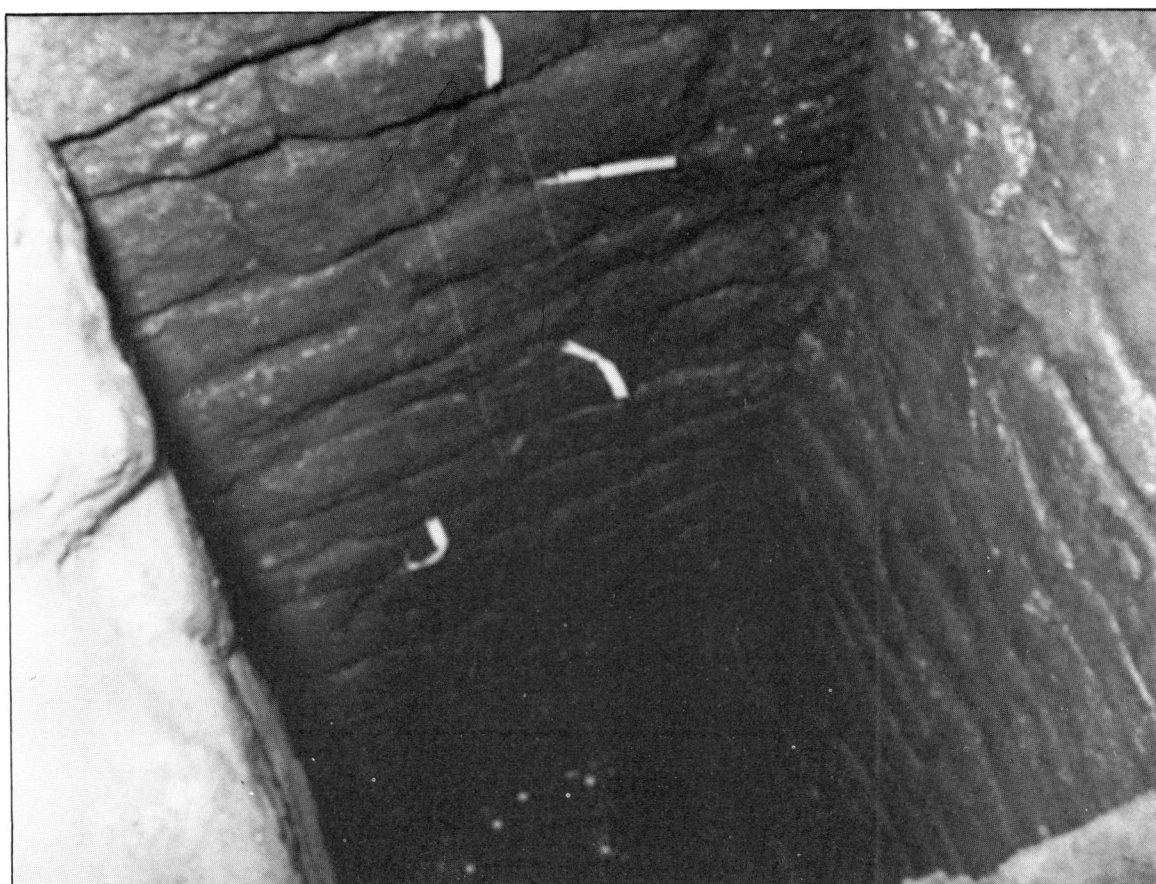

hills in check. Derventio, like all permanent military establishments throughout the ages, attracted tradesmen and Derby's first shops would have been here. It takes only a little imagination to stand on City Road and picture the comings and goings of the Roman legionary, clad in a kilt-like uniform with cloak, spear and round shield. Further along the banks of the Derwent, where today's young men play football in Darley Fields, a small village of native Britons had sprung up, supplying the Roman fort with servants and even slaves. In the forest, away from the river banks, the soldiers would hunt or take part in military exercises, for early Derby was a garrison town.

For over three centuries — the same length of time from the reign of Charles II to the present day — the Romans maintained their watch at Derventio. But their empire was to fall and one day at the beginning of the fifth century, the garrison at Derventio mobilised and swung out through the gates to march south down Rykneld Street, withdrawn in a desperate attempt to save Rome from the barbarians. Although released from Roman occupation, the British had little about which

to rejoice. They fought amongst themselves and although some may have lived for a time in the deserted stone buildings of Derventio, the area returned to the creatures of the forest. For well over a century there was nothing to be heard but the howl of a wild pig or the call of a red deer.

In the second half of the sixth century, the Saxon pirates, who had been a thorn in the side of the Romans with their constant coastal raids, sailed up the Trent and completed their colonisation of this island. Germanic tribes from Schleswig-Holstein settled in the area and a small Saxon settlement grew up around the ruined walls of Derventio until a larger village was founded one mile south of Little Chester, as the Saxons called the former Roman fort. The name which the Saxons chose for their new village was Northworthy (*North enclosure*). Its northern edge was bounded by a line of earthen ramparts, following an approximate line with the present St Alkmund's Way, and its southern limit may have been around the Cathedral and St Mary's Gate, while a separate development grew up around St Werburgh's church.

Roman pot duck's head aquamanile and brooches found on Derby Racecourse.

The Saxon choice was an obvious one. Their hatred of the Romans meant that they gave Derventio and Rykneld Street a wide berth; their limited engineering skills meant that they could not ford the Derwent; and they were lowland folk and, unlike the early British, soon set about clearing the area of forest. The area around St Werburgh's was an ideal site with Markeaton Brook (still running, culverted under the wheels of twentieth-century buses and cars) and Bramley Brook. Nearby, a Saxon called Walda started a dairy farm and *Walda's Wick* (or farm) became the Wardwick — a Saxon street joining the farm to Northworthy and a name which has lived for well over 1,000 years.

The embryonic city of Derby was born. The Saxon thane built a hall roofed with oak shingle from Spondon (*Spon = shingle; don = hill*), and fields were laid out for cultivation, one of which was Darley Field. On Sinfin (*broad fen*), Saxons snared ducks and geese in the low, hazy marshes. Hand mills or querns were brought from the stone at *Quarndon*, and many more Derby suburbs owe their present names to the Saxons.

Allestree was *Ethelheard's tree* — probably a tall oak marked his land — and Chaddesden belonged to *Ceadd* who found his home in the *den* or valley. Boulton was *Bola's* village and Alvaston belonged to *Alhwald*, while *Macca* lived at Mackworth and *Braegd* at Breadsall.

Northworthy became part of the kingdom of Mercia and like the Romans before them, the Saxons enjoyed 300 years of uninterrupted rule until they, too, were subject to attack from invaders sailing up the Trent. In AD868, the Danes captured Nottingham, although it was a further six years before Guthram sacked the Mercian capital of Repton and put King Burhred to flight before installing Ceowulf II as a puppet ruler. The Saxons retreated south across the Trent and the Danish takeover was complete.

The Danes knew that while the town on Markeaton Brook was good enough for the Saxon farmer, they had to defend its southern slopes from a Saxon counter-attack. Quickly, they constructed earthworks at Normanton (*Northmen's town*), whence they had a commanding view over the Trent valley,

Roman pig of lead found near Yeaveley. Inscribed: SOCIORVM LVTVD and BRIT EXARG. Product of Lutudarensian partners. British Lead from the lead/silver works.

including the ford at Twyford where the Saxon road crossed the river to Repton.

Northworthy became Derby. The name was chosen either because it means 'The place of the deer' (*Djur* in old Norse means 'deer' and *by* means 'place'); or the suffix 'by' was added to a contraction of the Roman name Derventio — which itself is taken from the Celtic name for the river and which would mean that the origin of the name Derby is lost in the mists of time. The town became part of the Danelaw, one of the semi-autonomous Five Burghs, and the Danes expanded further south into the Market Place, although the names of Iron Gate and Sadler Gate do not mean that Derby ever had city walls. 'Gate' is simply the Danish word for 'street'.

For many years the Danes had little to fear from the Saxons, a few of whom remained around the now ruined church of St Alkmund's. Alfred the Great had failed to reunite the kingdom and it was his daughter, Princess Aethelflaeda, who eventually countered the Danes with a series of daring raids along the slopes of the Trent valley. A great woman general who recovered a large amount of territory and who ranks alongside Boadicea, she was known as The Lady of the Mercians, and by later English historians as The English Joan of Arc, always leading her troops into battle on horseback.

Just before dawn on an August morning in AD917, Aethelflaeda led her Saxon hordes up the slopes towards Normanton where, according to a Saxon chronicler, she lost four officers in bitter hand-to-hand fighting before retaking Derby for the Saxons. The Danes fled north and for 26 years, Derby lay on the edge of an uneasy peace before the Danes attacked again in 943. Derby was regained by the Saxons the following year but eventually fell back into Danish control. In 1016, Canute finally united the kingdom and in Derby, Dane and Saxon lived together.

Derby's association with the Danelaw was a profitable one. When the Danes invaded Mercia in AD874, Repton was the capital of the kingdom and Northworthy was an unimportant settlement. Today, Repton is still a sleepy village, while the first stage of Derby's success story began with the Danish influence. The town became a royal borough, owned by the Danish crown, and in the year before the Norman Conquest, its 243 citizens (*burgesses*) each paid £24 tax, two-thirds to the king, one-third to the earl, the tax being collected by the king's representative, the reeve. The total population of Derby at that time has been estimated at about 1,200, including workers and their families. Certainly, Derby was a bigger town than Nottingham.

In September 1066, a coastal landing some 200 miles south would have worried the farmers of Derby far less than the impending harvest. But Derby blood was undoubtedly spilt under the banner of King Harold, first when he recruited on his rush north to engage his brother Tostig at the Battle of Stamford Bridge, and then on his way back to Hastings. When William's conquest was complete, Derby felt the changes it brought. Godwin's Kedleston was handed over to Gilbert, and later to Richard de Curzon, the son of a Norman knight; the Saxon Earl, Siward, lost

Plan of Little Chester by William Stukeley, who drew up this plan of the Roman settlement after visiting the site in 1721. He recorded finding part of the wall and ditch.

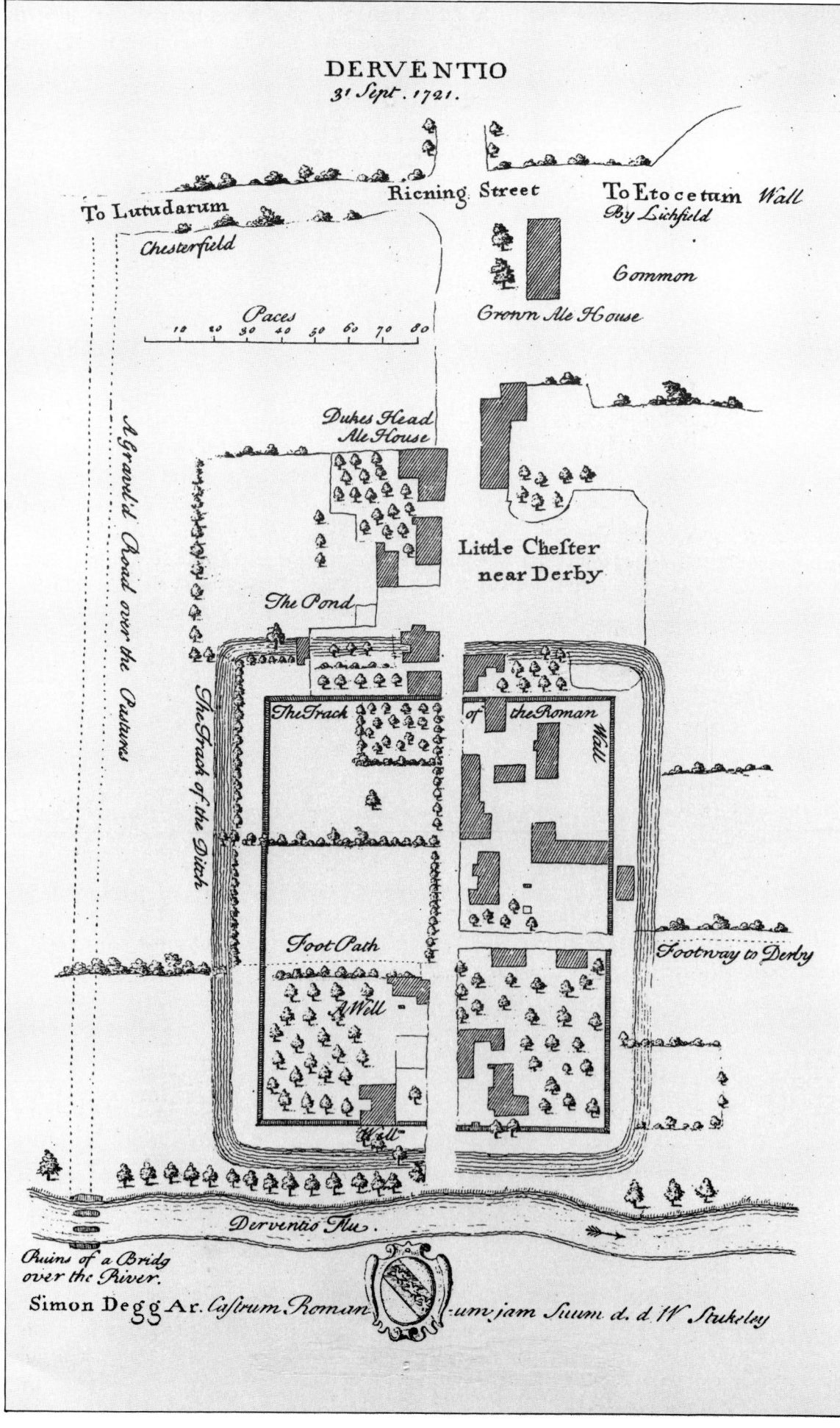

Markeaton, Allestree and Mackworth to Hugh, later Earl of Chester, and many churches and houses also changed hands.

Norman-French became a familiar tongue in Derby Market Place and from Kedleston, the lordly figure of Richard de Curzon, in helmet and chain-mail, rode into Derby to dark mutterings from the townsfolk. In the 20 years following the Conquest, Derby lost half its population and one-third of its houses, either through war losses, dwindling trade, or sheer panic as the townspeople fled the invader's path.

In 1086, four distinguished men rode into the town — Remiguis, Bishop of Lincoln, Walter Gifford, Earl of Buckingham, Adam of Rye and Henry de Ferrers, later Earl of Derby. They set up an office, probably in the nave of All Saint's, to conduct the first census. Derby was about to become the latest entry in Domesday Book. It appears that the town was a self-contained agricultural community, grinding its own corn, fattening its own livestock, shaping its own crude farm implements and weaving its own cloth, and even catching its own fish from the Derwent and eels from Sinfin. The town paid an increased tax to the new king of £30 per burgess per annum, and the manor of Litchurch was added to Derby's taxable account. At Duffield, Earl Ferrers built a castle which rivalled the Tower of London in size, although the legends of a former Saxon castle off London Road are probably wide of the mark. The land is known as Castlefields and this gives rise to conjecture that a castle once stood there. But there has never been any evidence — either material or documentary — and it is most likely that it was either the derivation of another word, or else a family name.

From Saxons to See

THE ecclesiastical story of Derby goes back to Anglo-Saxon times before reaching its culmination in 1927 with the establishment of the Diocese of Derby and Derbyshire, with the See of the Bishopric in Derby itself and with the choice of All Saints' as the cathedral of the new diocese.

Four of the six Derby churches mentioned in the Domesday Book survive today — All Saints', St Werburgh's, St Peter's and St Michael's — although the future of St Michael's is uncertain and the church itself has been declared redundant as a place of Anglican worship. Of the two other Domes-

Part of the Norman cross-shaft of St Alkmund's Church.

day churches, St Mary's is long gone, and the romantic St Alkmund's disappeared under a major road redevelopment in 1967.

The Domesday record of Derby's churches reads as follows:

'There was one church in the king's demesne with seven clerks who held two carucates of land freely in Cestre (*Little Chester*).

'There was also another church, similarly the king's belonging to which six clerks held nine bovates of land likewise freely in Corun and Detton *(Quarndon and Little Eaton)*.

'Geoffrey Anselin has one church which belonged to Tochi.

'Ralph, son of Herbert, has one church which belonged to Levric with one carucate of land.

'Norman, of Lincolia, has one church which belonged to Brun.

'Edric there has one church which belonged to Coln, his father.'

No dedications are mentioned, but it is generally accepted that All Saints' and St Alkmund's were the churches belonging to the King. There was another ancient church dedicated to St James but it is far from certain whether it was standing at the time of the Norman Conquest. The theory that this church and not St Mary's was the sixth Domesday church, and that St Mary's was actually a forerunner of All Saints', has no evidence to support it, save the mere fact that All Saints' faces directly down St Mary's Gate.

The origins of All Saints' are not recorded but it may be that the church was founded by King Edmund about 943. After the Domesday survey, All Saints' history is again a blank until the early years of the twelfth century when Henry I gave the church to Lincoln Cathedral. For some time, All Saints' enjoyed an unusual status as a collegiate

church, being 'royal and free' and exempt from the authorities of the Bishop of Lichfield and Coventry, in whose diocese it was then situated, and from the Archdeacon.

Today, All Saints' splendid sixteenth-century tower, built in the reign of Henry VIII, is as characteristic of Derby as St Paul's is of London. At 174 feet high it is the second-highest tower to be built for an English parish church, and was completed about 1530. It was incorporated in the present building which was rebuilt in 1725 when the

Top: *All Saints' Church from St Mary's Gate* Bottom: *The Archbishop of Canterbury, preaching in All Saints' on the Derby Infirmary Anniversary of 1897.*

piece of its kind, stretches across the entire length of the building. All Saints' also houses the tomb of the redoubtable Bess of Hardwick — Elizabeth, Countess of Shrewsbury, founder of the Cavendish family whose head is the Duke of Devonshire of Chatsworth House.

As the surviving Saxon church, St Werburgh's in Cheapside was Derby's oldest site of Christian worship still in use, although it is now a shopping arcade. Dedicated to St Werburgha, granddaughter of the great Mercian King, Penda, and the first Christian princess of Mercian birth, St Werburgh's was built about AD700. The permanent church no doubt followed the earliest baptisms in the running water of Markeaton Brook. The portable altar was eventually covered, thus ensuring the site as holy ground ever since. St Werburgh's has been rebuilt several times after floods and gales and the present building except the tower (1601) dates from 1894. An entry in the marriage register of 1735 records the wedding of Dr Samuel Johnson to Elizabeth 'Tetty' Porter.

A century after St Werburgh's was founded, the Danes slew Alkmund, son of King Alfred of Northumbria. Thereafter, Alkmund was worshipped as a martyr and a saint and his body was taken from its grave at Lilleshall in Shropshire, and brought to Northworthy for safe keeping. The saintly remains were laid to rest by a well which became known as St Alkmund's Well, and the shrine and church soon followed.

Derby became a centre for pilgrims and even after the Reformation, it is recorded that 'North-countrymen enquire upon his tomb and rest their packs upon it'. Many felt that the legend became fact in 1967 when St Alkmund's was razed to the ground. Four feet beneath its floor workmen found a heavy stone coffin, weighing almost one ton. Some felt that it was prepared for the remains of St Alkmund, before his body was finally placed near an altar, probably in the twelfth or thirteenth century. Others that it held the remains of an elder.

St Michael's stands midway between All Saints' and the site of the former St Alkmund's, on the northern slope of the central artery which links north with south. Indeed, if St Mary's stood where every clue seems to

mediæval church was pulled down. The new All Saints' was designed by James Gibb, already renowned for his St Martin-in-the-Fields and Oxford's Radcliffe Library.

Inside All Saints' Robert Bakewell's magnificent wrought-iron screen, a master-

St Werburgh's Church before it was rebuilt in 1894, showing the building of 1699.

A lithograph by W. Wood, showing the old mediæval church of St Alkmund's which was demolished in 1844.

place it, then this cluster of four churches was certainly Derby's ecclesiastical quarter — a common theme in Danish England.

St Michael's was apparently the Domesday church belonging to Geoffrey Anselin, who was lord of the dependent manor of Alvaston. Like many churches, St Michael's fell into utter disrepair over the centuries and in 1650, a Parliamentary Commission declared it fit only to be disused; by the end of the century, the churchyard was being used as a Corporation reservoir. For most of the eighteenth century, St Michael's was united with St Werburgh's and only in 1856, when

the gable end of the chancel collapsed, did the parishioners rally round and the church was completely rebuilt.

In the last century, St Michael's had a long list of distinguished vicars — men with a social awareness ahead of their times — and the church has one fascinating claim to fame as the first in England to produce a parish magazine. Sadly, the doors are now locked and barred and the debate over the future of the building goes on.

St Peter's Church originally served a small hamlet and stood alone in the southern half of mediæval Derby, in marked contrast to the four churches grouped on the northern heights. St Peter's is probably the Domesday church belonging to Levric in the time of Edward the Confessor, and afterwards to the Norman lord, Ralph, son of Herbert. St Peter's has more ancient remains than any other church in the city and parts of it date from norman times, although most is of the fourteenth century.

On St Mary's Bridge spanning the Derwent is one of England's few surviving bridge chapels, dedicated to the Virgin Mary. Built in the Middle Ages, the chapel provided travellers with a last opportunity to pray for

St Michael's Church showing the mediæval building before it was rebuilt in 1857.

a safe journey. A chaplain conducted these services and a 'bridge hermit' lived there, collecting the tolls and depending on alms from passers-by.

The Domesday Book recorded no monasteries in Derbyshire; yet within a century of the Norman Conquest, there were no less than eight in Derby itself. The name of the first one to be built lives on today in St Helen's House, formerly Derby School and now the headquarters of the local Workers' Educational Association. A Derby citizen named Tovi owned the land on which St Helen's House now stands, and in 1137, he gave the land — on which stood a holy well — to build a chapel or oratory there, dedicated to St Helen.

This done, the people of Derby felt that the Oratory was too small for the town and the monks were given further land at Darley, on the banks of the Derwent, where they constructed a much bigger monastery. Earl Ferrers was an enthusiastic supporter of the plan, and he gave the monks his churches at Uttoxeter and Crich, as well as some land at Ockbrook and the perpetual right to send a daily cart to Duffield and Chaddesden to collect timber. The monks were also given the incomes of St Peter's and St Michael's and in 1148 work began, to clear the thickly wooded hillside at Darley.

Today, we know the area as Darley Abbey, but in the twelfth century it was Derby Abbey and its first abbot was Albinus, who was elected in the chapter house before attending services in the abbey church and later having the bell ropes placed in his hands as a sign of his authority.

Within one hundred years, Derby Abbey owned land throughout the county, and in Derby itself, citizens great and small gave what they could. Ralph, a Derby saddler, gave the monks some land near Markeaton Brook, while Ralph FitzRalph gave up part of his rent of Alvaston Mill to help buy wine for the sacrament. Derby Abbey was a great establishment, housing monks, servants, farmworkers and labourers, and playing host to a great number of nobles and bishops — and even the king — as well as feeding the poor of Derby who gathered at the abbey gates each day.

A handful of monks were left at the original Oratory of St Helen's, which became St Helen's Hospital (a hospital then was a place which offered food and shelter to weary travellers). A Derby man named Waltheof founded a small priory of St James with a hospital attached, and St James' Lane (our St James' Street) was connected to the Wardwick by a bridge over Markeaton Brook where the monks levied a toll. St Leonard's Hospital was built outside the town on Osmaston Road (Leonard Street) to care for

lepers, although the establishment provided for only two monks and two lepers, so the dreadful disease was hardly rampant in Derby.

The county's only nunnery was at King's Mead *(King's Meadow)*. The Benedictine Nunnery of St Mary de Pratis was founded in 1160 by the Abbot at Darley, but it had a varied history. Henry III granted the Derby nuns one hundred shillings per annum to say prayers for the soul of his father, King John, but in 1328 the nunnery had fallen into debt. In 1393, the nuns received the gift of a house, three acres of meadow and 35 acres of pastures — later known as Nun's Green — but in 1400, a fire destroyed the document granting them the one hundred shillings from the Nottingham Crown Rent. Fortunately, the nuns acted quickly and obtained a new charter from Henry IV before the authorities at Nottingham discovered that the valuable document had been lost.

A new religious force found its way to Derby during the latter half of the thirteenth century when the Dominican Friars, or Blackfriars, with their black cloaks and begging bowls, established themselves. The friars, like the monks, were unmarried, but instead of living in monasteries, they travelled from town to town, preaching in the common tongue, not Latin, and bringing religion to everyday people. The passage of time brought the friars gifts of land and property and they soon lost the image of paupers. At Derby they built themselves a fine friary, on the site of the present Friary Hotel in Friar Gate.

The building was enlarged in 1319 and again in 1340. Each of the thirty friars had his own room or cell but, unlike the monks, they belonged to no particular establishment and the personnel were forever changing. The rumours of high living at the friary circulated from time to time and it was the last such establishment to be built in Derby.

The great religious and political upheaval of the Reformation which eventually gave birth to the Protestant Church, was felt in England during the sixteenth century when Henry VIII did away with the Pope's authority and proclaimed himself 'supreme head of the Church of England'. In Derby it meant that the town would lose its monasteries and in 1536, Thomas Cromwell, Henry's Chancellor, sent agents to take the surrender of St James' Priory. St Leonard's

St Peter's Church from the south-east. It is the only remaining mediæval church building in the city, although much restoration was done in the nineteenth century.

and King's Mead nunnery soon followed and then it was the turn of the bigger monasteries.

The Abbey at Darley was dissolved and the monks turned out of their houses and given pensions according to their rank, these pensions being assessed by Sir William Cavendish and Sir John Porte. Friar Laurens Sponar of the Friary signed the deed of surrender in the presence of Cromwell's representative, Dr John London, and the building became a private house belonging to one John Snape, 'gentleman'. The religious orders disappeared from Derby's streets, the monasteries were taken down and their valuables removed until there was little evidence that Derby had once been an important religious centre.

In the ensuing eras, Derby saw both sides of harsh religious persecution. During the short reign of Queen Mary, there was a return to the Catholic church and this led to a chapter in Derby's story, quite unequalled in its horror. Joan Waste, the 21-year-old blind daughter of a Derby baker, was found guilty of heresy. She was tried by Ralph Barnes, Bishop of Lichfield, who, it must be said, did his best to convince the authorities that the girl who preached the New Testament to the prisoners at Derby's gaol, was harmless enough. But the role of a broad-minded bishop was not a healthy one to play and eventually the dreadful writ 'De heretico comburendo' was issued.

On 1 August 1556, led by the hand of her brother, young Joan Waste began the awful journey from All Saints', through the town, and up to the Windmill Pit on Burton Road where she was burnt at the stake. As the flames engulfed her frail young body, she prayed to Christ. A few years ago, a landslip

Old house in Amen Alley, photographed in 1882 from Full Street. Mass books and breviaries were sold here for use in nearby All Saints' Church.

on Mill Hill Lane sent tons of earth crashing into the site of the Windmill Pit, giving rise to legend that the soul of Joan Waste still haunts the place where she met her dreadful death.

With the accession of Elizabeth I, two years after Joan Waste's death, the Church of England again became dominant and Derby was particularly notorious for mercilessly harrying *recusants* as Elizabeth called the Catholics. The grimmest case concerned three Roman Catholic priests — Richard Sympson, Robert Ludlam and Nicholas Garlick — who were hanged, drawn and quartered on 25 July 1588 with their severed limbs being hung up on St Mary's Bridge until 'two resolute Catholic gentlemen' removed them during the night and buried them in secret.

Mary, Queen of Scots, was involved in

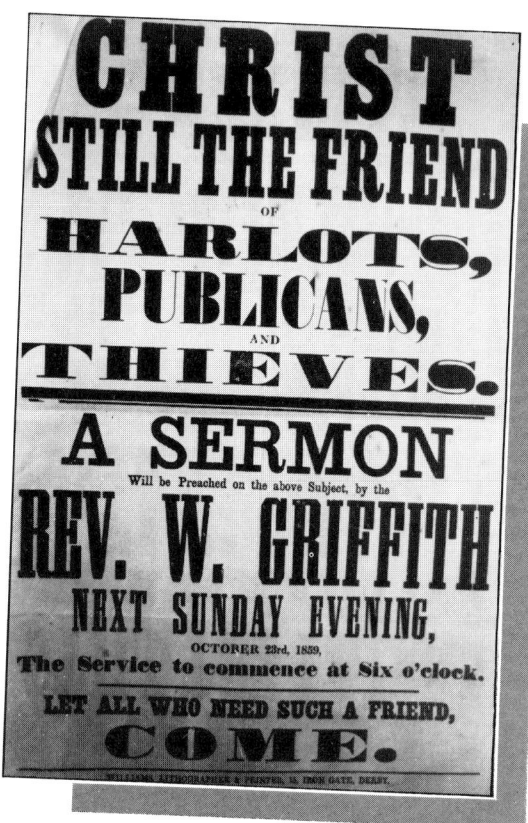

several plots to inspire a Catholic uprising and this most tragic figure in British history spent one night in Derby in January 1585, on her journey to imprisonment in Tutbury Castle. Her coach rolled over St Mary's Bridge and into a Derby strangely deserted as Bailiffs Robert Wood and Thomas York were ordered to clear the streets. Mary spent the night at Babington Hall and her gaoler, Sir Ralph Sadler, complained of being kept awake all night by the Derby watchmen calling the hour underneath his inn window.

Derby continued to feel the religious upheavals of the nation's story. The Parliamentary victory in the Civil War saw the Puritans level the chancel floor of All Saints' and remove all stained glass and pictures from Derby's churches. Presbyterians held sway in the town for a while and the term 'Quaker' was coined here.

In 1651, George Fox, founder of the Society of Friends, marched into a Derby 'steeple house' as he called the church, and interrupted the sermon. He was arrested and sentenced to twelve months' imprisonment, though not before he bade the magistrate, Gervase Bennett, to 'tremble at the word of the Lord'. Bennett called him a 'quaker' and the name stuck. Fox was paroled in the hope that he would leave the town, but he preached in Derby until his death and the city still has a Quaker meeting house.

Religious dissent also touched Derby and in the summer of 1790, the *Derby Mercury* announced: 'The Revd John Wesley intends preaching at his Meeting House in St Michael's Lane on Friday next'. In 1818, his followers moved to a chapel in King Street, and there followed Primitive Methodists, Baptists, Unitarians, and a whole host of other persuasions, each adding their own churches, chapels and meeting houses to the town's architecture. The Established Church, too, began to rebuild its old churches, adding new ones in the parish suburbs. In 1839, St Mary's Roman Catholic Church was opened. One of Pugin's finest buildings, it rose a few yards away from the anicent shrine of St Alkmund.

Politics and Power

FOR over 1,000 years, Derby has been a royal borough and citizens have long enjoyed the rights of local government. Although the earliest records are few, Derby was governed by its burgesses, probably through an elected council, with the reeve acting as chief officer, a link between the burgesses and the king.

The burgesses held their own courts to settle criminal and civil cases originating within their boundaries, while the new royal borough had a social system which differed from the old Saxon Northworthy, where there were simply the thane and the ordinary villagers. In Derby the burgesses — mostly tradesmen and master craftsmen — were the citizens with civil rights; the priests held a professional status as lawyers and officals, and the common herd of labourers, servants and apprentices enjoyed little or nothing in the way of civil rights.

Little is known about this early form of local government in Derby until Henry II (1154-89) gave two written charters to the burgesses of the town. An extract from one reads: 'I enjoin that the burgesses of Derby shall have their laws and their customes, as well as they best had them in the time of Henry, my grandfather, and William, my great-grandfather.'

By far the most important of Derby's early charters was the one bestowed upon the town by King John in 1204. It cost the burgesses over 60 marks and two horses, but in return they had their existing privileges renewed, as well as enjoying some valuable additions to their rights. The main provisions of this and subsequent charters of 1229 and 1256 were:

(i) Subject to royal confirmation, the burgesses were allowed to elect their own chief officer who was restyled Bailiff in 1256 and who was the forerunner of the present-day Mayor of Derby. The election was held annually on 29 September and the Bailiff was responsible for collecting fees, tolls and other dues before paying the king his share at Easter and Michaelmas.

(ii) After living in Derby for a year and a day, no man could be made a slave, save in the king's service, and any slave from outside the town could win his freedom by escaping capture in Derby for that period.

(iii) The burgesses were given the monopoly of cloth dyeing within a ten-mile radius of Derby.

(iv) Markets could be held twice-weekly and no man except the king could seize goods to repay a debt.

(v) The burgesses could impose tolls on boats crossing the Derwent, and tolls in the town markets, although they were themselves not liable to tolls in certain other towns.

Further charters followed. In 1327, Edward III granted the town a gaol; and in 1337, the same monarch allowed Derby to have two Bailiffs, so we must assume that the town's importance had grown during the previous century. The town's Merchants' Guild is also mentioned in various charters and we must also assume that it formed part of the Corporation. In 1283, Edward I seized the town charter after the Guild was alleged to have abused its privileges. Certainly, it did have an unfortunate reputation for rather tyrannical business methods but, as the charter was returned on payment of a fine, it could well have been an indirect method of increasing the flow of Derby money to the royal purse. The Corporation had already paid Henry III ten marks to expel the Jews from Derby. The only trade that Jews could practise in the Middle Ages was that of money lender and they were as unpopular in Derby as anywhere. The charter of Henry VI was granted in 1446 and gave Derby the right to

Top left: *Derby Town Hall in the Market Place. The upper storey was used by the Corporation for their meetings from the mid-fifteenth century to the building's demolition in 1730.*
Top right: *Derby Town Hall, 1730 to 1828.* Bottom left: *Derby Town Hall used from 1828 until its destruction by fire in 1840.* Bottom right: *The Guildhall lit up in 1935 for 100th anniversary of the Municipal Corporations Act.*

appoint a Borough Recorder who, with the two Bailiffs, formed a Commission of Peace to preside over the Court of Record.

In 1637, Derby received a charter from Charles I which proved to be the most significant since the one which John granted some four centuries earlier. Charles I's charter did away with the two Bailiffs and allowed Derby to have its own mayor. The last two Bailiffs to hold office were Henry Mellor and John Hope and it was Mellor, the senior of the two, who had the honour of becoming the first Mayor of Derby. The Town Council now consisted of the Mayor, ten Aldermen, 14 Brethren, and 14 Capital Burgesses or ordinary councillors. Derby Town Council continued in this form, with a few minor variations, until the Municipal Corporations Act of 1835 which provided for the election of councillors by all the burgesses, provided that they paid at least £10 in rates.

But in the seventeenth century, the Town

Council was a closed Corporation and once elected, a man was a member for life, or until he moved from Derby. Aldermen filled vacancies in their own ranks by choosing a Brethren; a Brethren was chosen by Aldermen and Brethren together choosing a Capital Burgess; and a vacancy in their ranks was filled by the whole Town Council electing a burgess. The system effectively gave complete powers of local government in Derby to the ten Aldermen.

Derby was also allowed a Lord High Steward who represented the town in the House of Lords — the first was the Earl of Devonshire; four honorary Chamberlains who collected the town's income; a Town Clerk who carried out the Town Council business; a Sergeant who carried the mace before the Mayor, and four Constables who 'guarded' the Mayor with short halberts, or battle-axes. Indeed, there was much ceremonial. The two silver maces which had belonged to the Bailiffs were made into one

town mace, and the Aldermen wore fur-trimmed long black gowns. The new Mayor was chosen by four Justices of the Peace — the current Mayor, the previous Mayor, and two senior Aldermen. On Michaelmas Day they all went to All Saints' and elected the Mayor, usually an Alderman who had not yet had the honour, before proclaiming their choice from the Market Cross.

More money was paid out to Charles II for a charter which allowed Derby to make its own by-laws, while in the reign of that monarch, in 1676, the town's income from rents, court fees and tolls came to just over £407, of which just over £400 was spent, including coal for the Guildhall, coats ordered by the Mayor, small repairs to town property and a small amount to the poor. Of the balance, half was spent on a civic dinner.

Municipal and Parliamentary reform was obviously long overdue and Derby, like many towns and cities, was overjoyed when the 1831

The wide west end of Friar Gate, formed by enclosing part of Nuns' Green following an Act of Parliament in 1768.

Left: *Sir Thomas
Roe, when Mayor of
Derby in 1897.*
Right: *Alderman
John Turner, Mayor
of Derby in 1879.*

General Election returned a Government which passed the Reform Bill by a large majority. They knew, however, that the House of Lords would not receive the Bill favourably and on Saturday, 8 October 1831, a large crowd in Derby Market Place learned that the Bill had indeed been overturned. Unease was widespread and the bells of All Saints', St Peter's and St Alkmund's were muffled and rang out until the early hours.

Meanwhile, rioting broke out and several shops and houses were damaged, among them, Chaddesden and Markeaton Halls. A similar plan to sack Kedleston Hall was aborted when someone remembered that a cannon was housed there. At 9am on Sunday, the Mayor held a meeting at the Town Hall where he refused to release three rioters arrested the previous night. The riot was sparked off again and the mob made for the Borough Gaol, formerly the County Gaol in Friar Gate, where they released 20 prisoners. They then went to the new County Gaol and after orders to disperse had been met with a hail of stones, the prison guards opened fire, killing a Derby man named Garner.

An uneasy peace was restored, although the MP Thomas Gisborne was howled down when he tried to address the rioters. That evening the rioters — by this time numbering some 1,500 — set off for the County Gaol again before being cut off by a troop of Nottingham Hussars. Throughout the night, the streets of Derby echoed to the crack of gunfire. Mrs Harrison's house on Chester Green was looted and around All Saints' a number of soldiers found themsleves under fire. One soldier was hit in the chest before his attacker was chased down King Street and shot in the thigh.

At noon on Monday, the Mayor, in an attempt to placate the mob, set up stalls in the Market Place so that a petition could be raised to send to the King. The stalls were smashed and eventually the Mayor read the Riot Act before the cavalry charged, killing a man named Hicking, who was shot. Not until two troops of yeomanry arrived from Leicester on Tuesday, was order restored, and the troops remained in Derby for a considerable time. In March 1832, a number of rioters faced trial at the Assizes. All but

Friar Gate Ward
ELECTION.

MESSRS. FORMAN & BRENTNALL

Will Address the Electors at the

Half Moon, Sadler Gate,

At 7 o'clock; at the

Waggon & Horses, Ashborne Road

At 8 o'clock; and at the

Brickmakers' Arms, Fowler St.,

At 9 o'clock.

THIS (THURSDAY) EVENING.

Derby, October 31st, 1861.

TO THE ELECTORS
OF
FRIAR-GATE
WARD.

GENTLEMEN,

We thank you cordially for honour you have conferred upon his day, in electing us by so large ajority.

We see in this result a proof that ral Principles are not, as some would have us believe, on the decline; and a justification of the course we took in asserting those principles in our former Address to you, and contesting the Ward on those grounds.

We trust that our conduct in the position in which you have placed us will justify your choice.

And remain, Gentlemen,
Your very obedient Servants,

**F. J. FORMAN,
C. BRENTNALL.**

Derby, November 1st, 1861.

two — who were each transported for seven years — were found Not Guilty. Serious rioting had also taken place in Nottingham and Bristol and in August 1832 the Lords finally passed the Bill.

In December 1833, a Royal Commission arrived in Derby and although its findings were not entirely satisfactory as far as the townspeople were concerned, it did accept that the Town Council was out of touch with the people it was supposed to represent. In 1835 the Municipal Corporations Act placed the election of the Town Council in the hands of ratepayers, abolishing the privileges of the exclusive band of burgesses. Derby's population at this time was 28,000 and an area of 1,796 acres was divided into six wards, each ward returning six councillors.

The first election under the new order took place on 26 December 1835, with each ward having its own polling booth in the Market Place. When the votes were counted it was found that the Whigs and the Radicals had the majority and on 1 January 1836, Joseph Strutt became the first Mayor of Derby under the new order, although the customary salary of £200 per annum and the right to mayoral dinners were discontinued. Derby became a County Borough under the Local Government Act of 1888.

Derby sent its first MPs to London in 1295 when Ranulph de Makeneye and John de la Cornere were elected to Edward I's 23rd Parliament — the first true English Parliament. They rode all the way to the capital on horseback. In Charles I's 'Long Parliament', during the prelude to the Civil War, William Allestree and Nathaniel Hallowes represented Derby, sitting with Cromwell's party. It was during the reign of James II that the Member for Derby was sent to the Tower of London. When James tried to readmit Roman Catholics to office, John Coke MP leapt to his feet crying, 'I hope that we are all Englishmen and that we shall not be frightened from our duty by a few high words.' Uproar followed and the Court Party shouted, 'Take down his words! To the Tower!'

To the Tower Coke went, but the mood of the country was on his side and he was no doubt confident, bearing in mind that the leader of the Opposition in the House of Lords was none other than the Earl of Devonshire. It was Devonshire who organised the campaign to overthrow James and

Edward VII raises his hat to a statue of his mother, Queen Victoria. The king unveiled the statue on The Spot before attending the Royal Agricultural Show at Osmaston Park in 1906.

Left: *King George V visiting an industrial exhibition at Derby in 1913.* Right: *A precarious perch for a woman in Derby Market Place as she waits for a glimpse of the Prince of Wales when he visited the town in 1932.*

offer the Crown to William of Orange. When William landed at Torquay in 1688, the Earl and 500 followers left Chatsworth for Derby, calling on the townsfolk to join the 'Glorious Revolution'. Mindful of Judge Jeffries and his 'Bloody Assizes', Derby men kept a low profile until they saw that William had a firm hold on the throne.

The scandal of 'pocket boroughs', whereby the Lords controlled the House of Commons vote, was felt strongly in Derby where the Whig Duke of Devonshire held the nomination for Derby 'in his pocket'. In 1742, the Pole family of Radbourne lost an election to the Cavendish nominee but contested the result with a charge that undue influence had been used to secure votes. They withdrew the claim as the Mayor, Aldermen and some local businessmen were on their way to London to give evidence.

In 1776, Derby was the subject of the infamous 'Election Trial' when the result was overturned after allegations of bribery. John W.Gisbourne, the Devonshire nominee, beat the Tory candidate, Daniel Parker Coke of Melbourne, by just 14 votes. The Tories' allegations were found proven by a House of Commons Committee of Inquiry and on 9 February 1776, an express rider reached Derby with the news that Coke was the new MP. Church bells greeted Coke when he arrived in the town six days later. Over 100 witnesses had travelled to London through a blinding snowstorm to back up tales of bribery carried out by the Mayor in Gisbourne's favour.

Derby also saw the awful culmination of 'England's Last Revolution', when a band of Derbyshire men set out to overthrow Parliament and set up a republic 'on the American system'. In June 1817, as the men were en route from Pentrich to Nottingham, where they were supposed to meet up with a large army from the north before setting out for London, they were intercepted by a troop of Hussars and fled. The leaders were eventually arrested and brought to Derby to stand trial for High Treason at the old County Hall in St Mary's Gate.

The proceedings had all the trappings of a State trial and when it was over, three men were sentenced to be hanged, drawn and quartered. They were Jeremiah Brandreth, 31, framework knitter of Sutton-in-Ashfield; Isaac Ludlam, 51, stonegetter of South Wingfield, and William Turner, 46, stonemason of South Wingfield. Eleven men were sentenced to be transported for life, three transported for 14 years, and a further six imprisoned for periods of between six months and two years. The men were hanged at Derby on Friday, 7 November 1817 and their bodies left dangling for an hour before being cut down and decapitated. The executioner was a burly Derbyshire miner and the huge crowd outside the gaol groaned and swayed as he held up Brandreth's head, saying 'Behold the head of the traitor Jeremiah Brandreth'. The men were not quartered but put into rough wooden coffins and buried in St Werburgh's churchyard.

The grim spectacle had a bizarre sequel when a ghost was reported in St Werburgh's churchyard, floating between the gravestones and carrying its head under its arm. At length no one would venture through the churchyard at night until one brave fellow felled the 'ghost' with a stone. It was none other than Pegg, a local barber, complete with sheet and wig block. Pegg lost an eye as the result of his escapade and Brandreth's ghost was seen no more.

In Times of Conflict

FROM the Norman Conquest, Derby has heard the clash of cold steel and the eventual thunder of firearms far less than many cities and towns in England. Yet a succession of wars — both foreign and civil — has meant that men from Derby have served their country in every conflict from the field of Agincourt to the sands of the Gulf. Derby has sent its fair share of menfolk to do battle over the centuries, whilst its citizens, too, have faced the nightmares of civilian bombardment from the air. Derby knows only too well about war.

Edward III began the disastrous Hundred Years War against the French and when Richard, Lord Grey of Codnor, rode into Derby in 1415 at the head of 162 bowmen and 60 lancers on his way to serve Henry V at Agincourt, it is unlikely that he left without at least a few local recruits. At any rate, the war was a profitable one for the smiths of Irongate who could not produce enough weapons for a war intended to conquer France and which ended with England losing every part of that country she had ever owned, except for Calais.

The Wars of the Roses saw Derby line up with the House of Lancaster, for the Duchy of Lancaster owned a large area of the county. One thousand Derbyshire men rallied to support Nicholas Longford when he raised the Red Rose standard at Longford in 1453 and marched to Derby. He came to take one of the town's few Yorkist sympathisers, one Walter Blount of Elvaston Hall. Blount was at the Friary when Longford entered Derby and after assaulting him, the Lancastrians marched through the Market Place, where they ignored orders to disperse from the High Sheriff, Sir John Gresley, and went on up the London Road to plunder Blount's Elvaston estate.

Nicholas Longford and his Derbyshire allies were arrested when the Yorkists gained their early victory and a special court in Derby, attended by Richard, Duke of York, the Protector while Henry VI was temporarily insane, found them guilty of high treason, although they were afterwards pardoned by the King. Eventually, the outcome of the Battle of Bosworth Field on 22 August 1485, when Henry of Richmond took the crown from Richard III, saw that Derby had taken the correct side.

There is no record of how Derby heard of the defeat of the Spanish Armada, although at the beginning of the reign of Elizabeth I, the town provided two archers and three billmen for the defence of Derbyshire. Twenty years earlier, in 1539, the muster for the town itself had numbered ten mounted archers, 39 unmounted archers, 56 mounted billmen and 126 unmounted billmen. In 1569 it was reported that Derby was slow to take up the new arquebus — a primitive firearm which took a long time to make ready — and only part of the town's defensive forces had been issued with it.

When the Stuart kings tried to enforce loans from the citizens, Derby was one of the towns strongly on the side of Parliament and when Charles I tried to reintroduce the ancient tax of 'ship money' — under an old decree, all ports had to provide a ship in time of war and Charles attempted to extend the tax to inland towns — Derby, Chesterfield and Wirksworth found themselves liable to provide a ship of 350 tons, as well as pay the wages for a 140-strong crew, and find food and ammunition.

The man deputed to collect this highly unpopular tax was the Sheriff, Sir John Gell of Hopton. In September 1635, Sir John told the Secretary of State that he was having great difficulty in collecting the tax and complained of 'the ill example which Derby is setting other towns', adding that in his opinion, the 'very many rich men' of Derby could well afford £250 or even £300 instead of the £120 demanded. The result was that the tax was raised to £175 and, after much haggling, paid over to Gell's successor, Sir John Harpur.

In August 1642 matters came to a head when the King raised his standard at Nottingham, collected an army, and the Civil War began. Charles marched to Derby, where he stayed three days, and 'borrowed' £300 from the town, together with a number of firearms, before continuing his march to the Welsh border, with some 20 Derby men who joined the royal colours. A gentleman's servant named Creswell tells how he escaped by climbing over a garden wall in St Alkmund's parish, crossing the Derwent at the weir at Darley, and making for Nottingham to join a troop of Roundhead horse.

Six weeks after the Cavaliers of Charles I had left Derby, Sir John Gell and his followers marched in from Wirksworth to set up Parliamentary headquarters at the Town Hall. Parliament had found a curious ally in the man who had tried to collect the despised ship money, and he became Governor of Derby and head of a Derbyshire force of some 15,000 men, of which Derby supplied 860.

The Civil War split the worthies of Derbyshire. Country gentry like the Curzons and Cokes of Melbourne fought with great vigour under the Parliamentary banner, whilst a few, like Sir John Harpur of Swarkestone, were for the Royalists. Once again, Derby's strategic position made it important as a garrison town, although the soldiers under Gell's command were held to be a rough and unscrupulous lot, unlike their Parliamentary force colleagues at Nottingham, and one writer calls them 'the most licentious, ungovernable wretches that belonged to the Parliament'.

From Derby, Gell went to the defence of Nottingham when it was attacked by the Duke of Newcastle, and his troops also sacked Bretby Hall and Wingfield Manor, won a victory over a superior number of Cavaliers

Above: *Sir John Gell, Parliamentary Governer of Derby during the English Civil War.* Left: *Exeter House, Derby, where Bonnie Prince Charlie made the decision to abandon his bid for the English crown.*

at Egginton, and captured the important Swarkestone Bridge. His tactics also included warding off Royalists as far afield as Leicester, Chester and Newark in a bid to keep the area around Derby free from the King's men. Once, in 1643 however, a party under the Earl of Newcastle almost reached Derby as Gell's men were, for once, forced

Peace celebrations in Derby's Rotten Row, when the Crimean War ended in 1856.

to retreat. In March of that year, at the battle of Hopton Heath, near Stafford, the Earl of Northampton was killed and his body interred at the Cavendish vault in All Saints' Church. At Uttoxeter, a trumpeter told Gell that the dead earl's son requested the return of his father's body, but when Gell responded with a claim for embalming charges and the return of weapons captured in the battle, the matter was dropped.

When the Civil War ended and England, Scotland and Ireland became a republican Commonwealth under Oliver Cromwell, Derby's garrison was sent to Ireland to 'serve Parliament against those bloudy rebels'. Although they had fought on his side, Derby's townsfolk hated the rule of Cromwell, the Protector, and when he died in 1658, it was recorded in the Latin notes of All Saints' parish register thus: 'Oliver Cromwell, the terror of England, died'. On Cromwell's death, Derby was recaptured for the Royalists by Colonel Charles White, once a Parliament man, but the Roundhead Colonel Saunders put White to flight without a drop of blood being spilled. Cromwell's protectorate did not last for long after his death and his son, Richard, was as unpopular in Derby, as his father had been. In 1660, Charles II was proclaimed King in Derby Market Place and the church bells rang out. Even Gell had campaigned for the restoration of the monarchy.

Derby was not through with days of dread and occupation. At 11 o'clock on the morning of Wednesday, 4 December 1745, two mounted soldiers trotted down Friar Gate towards the Town Hall. They found no one in authority and turned to Sadler Gate where they astounded the landlord of the George Inn with a demand for billets for 8,000 men. They were the vanguard of a rebel army marching on London to regain the Crown for the House of Stuart. Behind them came an ill-assorted band of soldiers and clansmen from the Scottish Highlands and in their midst, Prince Charles Edward Stuart, the Young Pretender, or Bonnie Prince Charlie, determined to regain the throne for his father.

Derby people knew that the Prince had returned from France and was marching south. When Carlisle fell, Derby's gentry began removing their property into the countryside and on 27 November, after a rider brought news that the rebels had reached Preston, troops drilled in Derby Market Place. On 3 December, joy at the rumour that the rebels were marching into the jaws of the Duke of Cumberland's army at Lichfield turned to horror at another message which confirmed that the Prince was, in fact, at Ashbourne and marching on Derby. After announcing their intentions to march north and take on the rebels, the local volunteer force, the Derby Blues, changed their minds and marched off to Nottingham at 10 o'clock that evening, leaving Derby's citizens to fend for themselves.

After the Prince's initial force had arrived in the town, their commander, Lord George Murray, rode to his quarters in the Market Place and throughout the afternoon hundreds of mounted troops clattered through Derby's streets, followed by a motley collection of clansmen. Towards dusk, the Young Pretender arrived. A handsome man of 25, he entered the Market Place on foot, wearing the Highland tartan and broadsword, green bonnet laced with gold, and a white wig. He marched briskly to his headquarters — the mansion of Lord Exeter in Full Street.

The following day, the town crier announced that all those due to pay government taxes must contribute to the Prince's funds. Refusal meant death and about £2,500 were raised. Local people were plundered of gloves, shoes and powderkegs and on Nun's Green a barn full of fodder was sacked. Writing in the next issue of the *Derby Mercury* one man described the six officers and 40 men who had descended on him as 'no better than a herd of Hottentots or wild monkies'.

Early on the evening of 5 December, a council of war was held in the oak-panelled drawing-room of Exeter House and towards midnight the voices became raised. The Prince was all for pressing on south in the hope that government troops would go over to him; Lord George Murray argued that such a tactic would be suicidal. Into the small hours the arguments and counter-arguments

Territorial soldiers march down London Road, Derby, in 1914 on their way to war. Many never returned.

raged until, at last, the Prince slumped in his chair in bitter disappointment.

On 6 December, a troop of horses was sent to Swarkestone bridge and ammunition handed out to aid the lie that the main body of rebels was going back north to meet reinforcements whilst Derby was held by the Swarkestone troop. At 9 o'clock that morning, the Prince left his Full Street headquarters and mounted a black charger. He rode it across the Market Place and down Sadler Gate into open country and exile once again. There was no market that day and on Sunday the churches remained closed with most of the clergy still hiding in the neighbouring countryside. The three days had been a frightening experience for Derbeians who were seething with anger.

When news of the Prince's defeat at Culloden on 16 April 1746 finally reached Derby, it was greeted with peals of bells.

Derby has greeted many national victories with its church bells. On 19 October 1759, the capture of Quebec was celebrated with bells and bonfires; and one month later the traditional peace of the Sabbath was broken when Derbeians learned of the destruction of the French fleet at Brest. In May 1763 the Treaty of Peace was received with silent prayers by French prisoners-of-war who left Derby for their homeland via Hull.

When the peace treaty between France, England, Spain and Holland was signed in 1802, two fat oxen — the gift of the Corporation — were roasted in the Market Place and distributed to the townsfolk together with 'many potatoes and several barrels of ale'. The 1814 peace between England and France was celebrated with a ball at the old Assembly Rooms, opening to the tune of *White Cockade*. Male inhabitants were given a dinner and females were handed 1s 6d each. There were buns and ale for over 4,000 children in the Market Place and the *Derby Mercury* reported: 'The lofty structures of Messrs Strutt's Cotton Mill and Messrs Cox's Shot Tower were linked with the threads of flowing ribbons representing the emblems of peace and plenty.'

After Napoleon's escape from Elba a few months later, Derby waited until well after the news of the battle of Waterloo before daring to celebrate. Not until they heard of the fall of Paris — the news reached Derby at 6 o'clock on Saturday, 8 July 1815 — did the townsfolk rejoice with celebrations to match the victory at Trafalgar some ten years earlier (although on that occasion the illuminations were extinguished at 11pm because of Nelson's death).

Derby has also sent its men bravely to war when the need arose and there will surely never be scenes to match those of Wednesday, 8 November 1899, when 214 officers and men of the Sherwood Foresters marched out of Normanton Barracks and off to the Boer War. They were the second batch of local men to answer the colours of Queen Victoria. As they wheeled down St Thomas' Road, Pear Tree Road and Normanton Road to the Midland Station, the rapturous cheers of thousands of people rung in their ears. The *Derby Daily Telegraph* commented: 'It was the chance of a lifetime to see one's fellow workers march off to fight for Queen and country.'

All police leave was cancelled and every vantage point was taken as the soldiers — wearing khaki for the first time — marched to the depôt's own drum and fife band, the local volunteer band, and another volunteer bugle band, playing tunes like *Say Au Revoir Not Goodbye* and *Listen to the Band*. At the station a troop train took them to Portsmouth and the troopship *Dunera*, although not before there were more wild scenes with the Midland Hotel becoming an emergency first-aid centre. On 15 June, news arrived of disaster to the 4th Derby Militia — 36 killed, 104 wounded, the rest captured.

Patriotism was still popular in 1914 as Derby men went to Flanders, only this time the war came much closer to home when a Zeppelin bombed the Locomotive Works. By the time Derby Market Place was again bedecked in red, white and blue in November 1918, there was not a street in the town which had not lost a husband or sweetheart, brother or son, in the most awful of wars. When the news of the Armistice came (crowds had been milling around the former *Evening Telegraph* offices in the Cornmarket for almost 18 hours) works and schools closed down immediately and schools stayed closed all week. At Derbyshire Assizes there was only momentary jubilation before Mr Justice Shearman apologised to counsel for interrupting his speech.

In September 1939, when German Panzers rolled into action against Polish cavalry, it became obvious that the 1914-18 sacrifice had been in vain and Derby girded itself for a second great war. This time there were to be 45 civilian deaths due to bombing and over 4,000 houses damaged or destroyed.

Amazingly, although it was the home of Rolls-Royce and the very nerve centre of the Merlin engine which powered the Spitfire, Derby received little attention from the Luftwaffe by comparison to cities like Coventry and Sheffield. Only once — on a dull, drizzly morning in July 1942 — did a lone German raider penetrate to Rolls-Royce.

Indian cavalry stationed at Markeaton Park during World War Two.

Members of the Air Cadet Defence Corps at Highfield House, Derby, in December 1940.

The daring pilot dropped four bombs and raked the works with machine-gun bullets, killing 22 and seriously injuring 40 in Derby's heaviest casualty list of the war. After fouling a balloon cable, the pilot made his getaway over Markeaton Park, telling German radio audiences later: 'We were all in good spirits at having succeeded.'

Derby contributed £1,688,358 to Wings for Victory and £1,942,657 to Warships Week which enabled the town to adopt the cruiser HMS *Kenya*. On foreign fields the Sherwood Foresters and Derbyshire Yeomanry distinguished themselves with service in every theatre of war and Derby men were at Dunkirk, El Alamein, Singapore, Anzio and

Normandy, as well as serving in the Atlantic convoys and as some of The Few in the Battle of Britain.

Since that second great war, the men of Derby have seen service in Korea with the UN force; in Kenya, in Aden and in Cyprus; in the Falklands and in the Gulf; and even today Derby sons endure the wretched urban war of Northern Ireland. For Agincourt read Bogside.

Normanton Barracks stands sad and neglected just before its demolition to make way for the Foresters Business Park in the late 1980s.

The Battle of Britain Window at Rolls-Royce's Nightingale Road site. The Merlin engine which played such a prominent role in the war for the air between 1939 and 1945 was developed and manufactured in Derby.

Murder and Mayhem

THE story of law enforcement and crime in Derby runs parallel with the story of law and order throughout England. Derby has had its fair share of celebrated murder trials; and the town was as guilty as any in meeting out horrific punishments in less enlightened times.

Henry III allowed Derby to have its own Coroner, thus freeing it from interference by the county; that particular monarch also gave Derby permission to erect its own gallows to hang local criminals. When Edward III allowed the town to have a gaol, Derby was self-sufficient in the punishment of law-breakers. And like the rest of England, Derby treated its criminals harshly. In the Market Place there were stocks in which offenders were often condemned to sit for hours while being pelted with rotten eggs and fruit. At Cuckstool's Mill, near St Werburgh's Church, scolds (or quarrelsome women) and tradesmen who broke the laws were immersed in Markeaton Brook by means of a ducking stool.

In the reign of Henry VI, Derby had a gaol with two cells in the Guildhall and when Henry VII was on the throne, two new gallows were erected in the town. In Elizabethan times, Derby was given its own sheriff (before then, Derbyshire prisoners were dealt with by the neighbouring Nottinghamshire prison authorities) and a county prison was built over a brook in Tenant Street. It was little more than a sewer and 'gaol fever' was soon rampant, killing several inmates; three of those who escaped that dreadful death were later killed in equally horrible circumstances when the brook flooded and they were drowned.

Still the horrible punishments continued. In 1586, several men and three women were flogged in Derby Market Place for trivial offences and in 1601, a woman who was found guilty of poisoning her husband was burnt at the stake in Windmill Pit on Burton Road. Even debtors found themselves at the mercy of unscrupulous gaolers. They were flung in prison and left there until they could pay both their debts and their board and lodging whilst inside. More than one gaoler rented out their cells to prisoners who could afford to pay more than the debtors. In the 1680s one William Wragg did just that and at the same time debtors complained about the awful bread which was supplied by a baker called Thomas Mee.

The Town Gaol at the Guildhall was so small that prisoners there were transferred to the county prison until a new Town Gaol had been built at Willow Row in 1756, but at Willow Row the prisoners fared little better and the new gaoler called Greatorex followed the custom of letting out the cells. On one occasion he was even locked in his own gaol for playing football but lived up to his boast that the prison could not hold him, and was free in one night. Two other prisoners who escaped were not so lucky and they were soon recaptured and heavily ironed. A man called Elder Clark was publicly flogged in the Market Place for stealing silk and John Clowne was sentenced to one hour in the Market Place pillory after a particularly petty offence.

Highwaymen are often pictured as romantic figures and the Derby area was at one time plagued by these masked riders who lay in wait for stage-coaches. They did not always find rich pickings and on one occasion it was reported that a highwayman who stopped the Derby coach felt so sorry for the poor state of his victims that he gave back a shilling to one man so that he could tip the driver.

In June 1737, it was reported that a man arrived at the King's Head Inn at Derby and told patrons that he had been robbed of his watch, some silver and £4 by no less a rogue than Dick Turpin at Egginton Heath. At that time, however, Turpin was being reported in several places at once. Nevertheless, the young man's audience would have hung on his every word at the mention of so infamous a name.

Even the town centre was not safe — in the eighteenth century there were no police and after dark it was often impossible to pick one's way through the pitch-black streets — and in October 1776 a tradesman called Ledsworth was riding along Osmaston Road when he was held at pistol-point by four footpads who threw him from his horse and robbed him of all his money. When a stranger came into Derby he was watched carefully and in January 1748, a gang of thieves caused havoc in Derby market. The penalties for stealing were still of an ultimate nature. In August 1755, Anne Williamson was hanged at Derby after being found guilty of picking pockets at Ashbourne.

The people of Derby were not safe, even in their own homes. Burglary was rife and one man was even awakened by thieves who were attempting to steal his bedclothes. In February 1751, thieves broke into the home of Revd Cantrell in St Alkmund's Church-yard and stole silk, clothing and tea; and in 1763 the *Derby Mercury* reported that one man ordered a tankard of ale at the Red Lion Inn, retired with it to his room, and lowered it out of the window on a piece of string, before bidding a brazen good evening to the landlord and making off into the night with his loot. In January 1792 night-watchmen were appointed to patrol Derby's streets — less than one month later, five guineas' reward was offered for information concerning an attack on the patrol when 'large stones were thrown'.

As the nineteenth century began, some of the crueller punishments were abandoned, although in 1825 a man was sentenced to the pillory in the Market Place for 'slandering his neighbour's wife', and only shortly before that, a man called Maddocks had robbed a pauper girl of what few groceries she

possessed and found himself dragged around the Market Place, tied to the tail of a cart while being whipped.

But the law enforcement authorities were now turning to the practice of deportation and many Derby people were sentenced to rot in the hulks that would take them to Australia. Eighteen-year-old William Hinkley was sent away for 14 years after he stole a ham from Robert Slater. Botany Bay became the dreaded destination and in May 1819, nine convicts were shepherded out of the County Gaol to be taken by coach to Sheerness and the appropriately-named *Retribution* which would take them to Australia. When the coach changed horses at Loughborough's Red Lion Inn, the men escaped, although still in fetters.

In 1821 a new County Gaol was opened in Vernon Street and even in the late 1980s, Derby's gamblers still went there — not to pay off their debts but to place bets, for the old County Gaol became Derby greyhound stadium in the 1930s, although from the outside it had hardly changed over the century. The Grecian-Doric styled building was designed by Francis Goodwin and cost

Top: *Moneypenny's view of the County Gaol in Friar Gate.* Bottom: *Derby's last gaol. It was demolished in 1928, save for the exterior, and is pictured here when greyhound racing was staged on the site from 1931 to the late 1980s.*

£65,227 to build. When it was opened, the Society for the Improvement of Prison Discipline called it 'the best plan and construction in the United Kingdom.' It housed 315 prisoners and had its own chapel, bakehouse, water reservoirs, tables and infirmary and was air-conditioned and centrally-heated by hot water. Male inmates spent the day in carpentry, smithing, shoemaking and tailoring; the female prisoners were kept busy washing and ironing.

It was the scene of many executions, both public and private, and was used as a civil prison right up to 1916, when it became a military prison before being sold in 1929. In the high summer of 1914, as Europe hurtled headlong towards war, the County Gaol in Vernon Street was the site of an extraordinary demonstration by the trade union movement when a frail Burton man, Vale Rawlings was imprisoned there for allegedly striking a policeman during a trade dispute at the Burton factory of Derby's F.W.Hampshire, then flypaper manufacturers. On Sunday, 28 June 1914, a huge crowd gathered outside the prison to sing the *Red Flag* and after questions were asked in Parliament and a petition was raised by Keir Hardie MP, Rawlings was released to a hero's welcome.

Over the years, the story of Derby has involved some celebrated murder trials and there are several which are worth recording here.

As the long winter night grudgingly gave way to dawn on the last Monday before Christmas 1774, a party of workmen trudged reluctantly down Full Street, hunching their shoulders against the chill December air. As they passed a large house they heard screams and, on entering, they found a hysterical woman servant and the body of an elderly woman, Mrs May Vickars. The many rings on Mrs Vickar's fingers had been brutally ripped off and the house ransacked. The servant blurted out her story: a man had robbed them and threatened to murder the maid if she raised the alarm. The girl had waited, terrified, until the first light when she managed to attract the workmen's attention.

Investigations brought a whitesmith called

The County Hall in St Mary's Gate dates from 1660 and was the scene of many murder trials and also the treason trial which resulted from the Pentrich Revolution.

Matt Cocklane under suspicion but there was no trace of him. It appeared that he had fled to Liverpool and there the trail might have ended, but for the sharp eye of an official in Dublin who spotted Cocklane in the Irish capital. Late one October night — ten months after the brutal murder — Cocklane was brought into Derby amid great excitement and in March 1776 he was found guilty of murder at the Assizes and sentenced to death. In the condemned cell at the County Gaol, Cocklane wrote down his confession. He had entered the house through a small back window and beaten Mrs Vickars to death with an iron pin before stealing her rings and £300-worth of gold. He made his escape along Full Street, All Saints' Churchyard and St Mary's Gate before crossing Nun's Green and heading for Ashbourne.

He was hanged before a large crowd and at the request of 'some gentlemen of the town', his body was not handed over to local surgeons for dissection, but was tarred and hung in chains at Bradshaw Hay — probably where the present-day Bradshaw Way meets London Road. His story did not end there. A wager struck in the Green Dragon in St Peter's Street saw one of the company climb up a ladder to offer Cocklane's corpse 'a basin of broth to warm up his bones'. As the clock struck midnight, the brash young man climbed the gibbet and held up the basin with the words, 'Matthew, you must be cold up there. Here's a basin of broth!' From the still night air a voice boomed back, 'Blow on it, then!' The daredevil fell off the ladder and fled along London Road. At the foot of the ladder his colleagues had installed Squeaking Jemmy, a local ventriloquist.

The last man to be publicly executed in Derby was Richard Thorley who met his untimely end outside the Vernon Street gaol on 11 April 1862; and it was the crucial evidence of a ten-year-old boy — the star prosecution witness — which sent him to the gallows and an unfortunate place in Derby's story. Over 20,000 people turned out to witness the sickening spectacle.

Young Charles Wibberly was playing in a court off Agard Street on a cold February evening in 1862 when, by the light of a flickering gaslamp, he saw Eliza Morrow, one of the residents, arguing with a man just before 8pm. The man was Thorley, a widower, who had formed a stormy relationship with Morrow, who lived with her lodger, Ann Webster, at Court No 4. On 12 February, Thorley visited the house and saw Morrow with a soldier who, it was alleged, she used, to make her lover jealous. Thorley went on a drinking spree and returned to the Morrow household twice — the first time causing such a commotion that Ann Webster called the police and had him removed.

On the second occasion, Thorley sent a message into the house that he wanted to see Morrow and the two stood in the court arguing. Thorley noticed some small boys and asked angrily 'What do you want?' The boys ran off but young Wibberly waited at the end of the alley. Seconds later there was a scream and Thorley rushed past Wibberly. Two neighbours, Urania Morrow and Emma Underwood came running to find Eliza propped up against the wall in a pool of blood with the most fearful wounds to her throat. As they helped her inside, young Wibberly cried 'Look, Mrs Underwood, a razor!' Emma Underwood carefully picked up an open cut-throat razor and took it into number 4.

Thorley, meanwhile, had run across Derby and into the Spa Inn in Abbey Street where he explained away the blood on his clothing as a result of a fight in the Abbey Inn. Under oath later, the Abbey Inn landlord, Thomas Rickard, swore there had been no trouble at his inn that night. Thorley left the Spa Inn some time after 10pm and was arrested in Canal Street by Detective-Sergeant Thomas Vessey. A local surgeon, Joseph German had been called to the Morrow house where Eliza died in his arms. Thorley now faced a murder charge.

At Derbyshire Assizes the evidence of the surgeon, lodger, two pub landlords and the neighbours, all pointed to Thorley's guilt. But it was young Charles Wibberly who stood up to the most intense cross-examination by Mr Yeatman for the defence, and swore that he had seen Thorley and Morrow struggle before the girl-dropped to the ground. Mr Justice Williams donned the black cap and passed sentence.

Thorley's execution was set for noon on 11 April and at 1am that day he wrote out a full confession. The prison chaplain asked him if he had any regrets. 'No', he replied, 'she got what she deserved'. At 9.30am the condemned service was held in Thorley's cell and just before noon the tolling bell announced that execution was at hand. Down in the prison Thorley said goodbye to his fellow prisoners with the words 'Let my sentence be a warning to you all'. Then Calcraft the executioner took off Thorley's neckerchief and looked for a pocket in which to put it. Thorley told him politely 'You'll find a pocket on the left side'.

The crowd — some of whom had walked miles to be there — were hushed as Calcraft put the noose around Thorley's neck and the condemned man turned his pale face to the sky, praying fervently before handing a small hymn book to one of the officials. After the execution his body was left to hang for one hour before being buried within the prison walls. Inside the hymn book he had written for his sister 'Hannah Brearley, with her brother Richard's dying love. April 11 1862'.

Of all Derby murder trials, perhaps the most celebrated was that of 23-year-old Gerald Mainwaring, who was sentenced to death in July 1879 after shooting Constable

Moss at Derby Lock-Up after being taken there for driving a horse and trap recklessly through the town. He had suddenly pulled out a revolver and shot Moss dead. At his trial Mainwaring, the son of a clergyman, who had recently returned from America, was found guilty after the jury had been out for nearly three and a half hours. Soon afterwards the *Derby Daily Telegraph* — within a few days of its first appearance — heard of rumours that the jury could not agree and had decided the verdict by ballot. With the jury locked at six in favour of a conviction and six for an acquittal, the foreman had cast his deciding vote in favour of a guilty verdict. The newpaper informed the Home Secretary and in view of the alleged irregularities, Mainwaring's sentence was commuted to life imprisonment.

When Sir Robert Peel authorised a police force in 1843, Derby's consisted of one superintendent and 20 constables, each paid 18s per week. It was the beginning of the force which is today part of the Derbyshire County Constabulary, a result of local government reorganisation which saw the end of the Derby Borough Police as a separate body.

Members of the Derbyshire Constabulary attend a traffic accident at Markeaton in 1931. Derby Borough Police was absorbed into the county force after local government reorganistion in the 1970s.

Lessons Learnt

THE origin of Derby's first school is not recorded, but there is little doubt that it was attached to one of the collegiate churches, probably All Saints', well before the Norman Conquest. Any Derby boy could enter the church and become a priest and at this early school he would be taught Latin, the language in which the services were held, and arithmetic to enable him to keep the church accounts. As only priests could read and write, he would also act as an official or lawyer, in addition to his duties as a clergyman. Thus, Derby had education for its sons over one thousand years ago.

In 1160, a local businessman named Walkelin gave up his house to the school. The classroom was situated in the main hall of the house and the master and a few priests used the bedrooms as a hostel. The schoolmaster was known as William Barbe Aprilas, or April Beard. Was that the nickname by which twelfth-century Derby boys knew their teacher? The only education available to girls was at the nunnery of St Mary's where daughters of some of the better-off Derby families learned to read and sew.

For centuries the pattern of education in Derby remained unchanged. In 1554, Queen Mary gave the town a free grammar school among the services to be maintained by her large grants to Derby. The Derby School known to generations of local boys was born, and it is reputed to have been the second oldest grammar school in the country. The original sixteenth-century schoolroom still survives in the shadow of St Peter's Church and after a local news agency stepped in to save the building and give it a new lease of life as their headquarters, it became the splendid Derby Heritage Centre in 1992.

Besides Derby School, a few private schools began to appear to educate the children of 'middle-class' Derbeians. In the 1740s, references to Dr Sylvester's school in Friar Gate appear; in 1789, a Mr Freer announced that he was giving up his school in St Peter's parish and recommended his successor and former assistant, Matthew Spencer (grandfather of Herbert Spencer). One year later, Matthew Spencer announced that 'his school is in the Green Lane where he instructs youths in Reading, Writing, Merchants' Accompts, Mensuration (with land surveying), Algebra, etc etc' and that 'he can accommodate a few gentlemen at his house'. The terms were one guinea entrance fee and 13 guineas per annum for board and education. On 1 October 1792, a girls' boarding school opened in All Saints' Churchyard where young ladies could learn English and needlework. The fees were the same as the Green Lane school except that the girls were asked to bring an extra half-guinea a quarter for laundry, a pair of sheets and four towels.

For working-class children the opportunities were severely limited and the only schools for them were at the homes of those few Derby citizens who wished to pass their own knowledge on to the citizens of the future. A man named John Pratt opened his school in Bridge Gate on 12 January 1789, teaching youngsters reading, writing and arithmetic. Later he opened the town's first night school, offering workers the chance to learn writing and arithmetic at threepence per week, or reading only at twopence per week.

Early in the nineteenth century, Joseph Lancaster, the Quaker, suggested a system of non-sectarian schooling, an idea which was quickly followed by a rival method under the umbrella of the Church of England, suggested by Dr Bell. Although Lancaster lectured in Derby on his idea in 1810, it was

The Tudor building which housed the original Derby School in St Peter's Churchyard. It is now the Derby Heritage Centre.

two years before any action was taken. In March 1812 — three years before the Battle of Waterloo — local clergy asked the Mayor of Derby to provide a school on Bell's idea. A month later, the Nonconformists founded a society to foster Lancaster's plan and a schoolroom and master, one John Adams, were provided in Full Street. In its first year,

373 children, using slates, attended the Lancastrian School, learning writing and arithmetic and reading the Scriptures. Adams was paid £75 per annum, and monitors (older children used as teachers) received £15 per annum each.

Funds were raised in three ways — by subscription (much of that coming from local gentry), by grants from the National Society for Lancastrian Schools, and by charging a monthly fee of twopence per pupil. In 1825, the Lancastrian School moved to a new building in Orchard Street. Shortly afterwards, a National School for 220 Church of England children opened its doors in Bold Lane, and in 1831, a British School for girls was opened in the George Inn Yard in Sadler Gate. Twelve years later, additional property was bought in Orchard Street and the Lancastrian Boys School and the British Girls School amalgamated under one roof as the Derby British School, later having its own infant class.

Derby School, meanwhile, had declined over the turn of the century and in 1813, when the assistant master died, he was not replaced because the pupils numbered so few. In 1827, there were only two pupils, and later just one master and one pupil. In 1840, Derby School was taken over by the Municipal Charity Trustees, and out of the Corporation's hands. Eventually the school recovered and in 1863 it moved from its old home in St Peter's Churchyard and into St Helen's House. In 1872, the Prince and Princess of Wales opened new rooms at Derby School and a happier chapter in the school's history began to unfold.

Despite financial difficulties, Derby's mid-nineteenth-century day schools struggled on, educating some 3,000 children. But some of the children from Derby's worst slums were considered too dirty and too neglected to be allowed into the schools. Eighty such children found their education at a 'Ragged School' which opened in Park Street.

Eventually, the Government decreed that all children should receive compulsory schooling and the setting up and maintaining of sufficient schools was entrusted to special committees. On 23 January 1871, ratepayers elected the Derby School Board

which included timber merchant (later Sir) Thomas Roe, three clergymen, a silk merchant, a draper, a lawyer and a coachbuilder, with William Cooper as its first clerk. After improving the existing schools, the Board set about building its own. The first Derby Board School was erected in Gerard Street. It was followed by many more of similar style. The Gerard Street school became Becket School after World War Two and was demolished exactly one hundred years after it first opened.

Other educational establishments began to open in Derby. In 1825, Revd E.Higginson opened the Mechanics' Institute in the Wardwick. If offered inexpensive science classes, a library and exhibitions to delight a Derby population fascinated by the ever expanding barriers of discovery. The Church of England started an Institute for the Training of Schoolmistresses — forerunner of Derby Training College — and the Derby School of Science and the School of Art, both founded in the late nineteenth century, spawned Derby Technical College.

After World War Two, Derby had two boys' grammar schools and two girls' grammar schools. Bemrose School was built in Uttoxeter New Road and opened in 1930 to replace the old Secondary Technical School in Abbey Street. It joined the ancient Derby School as a boys' grammar school. Parkfields Cedars was the older of the two girls' grammar schools, sited in a country mansion on Kedleston Road, and Homelands School for Girls completed the quartet, having been opened in 1939 on Village Street, Normanton, at a cost of £90,000. Central School was Derby's one secondary technical school — between grammar and secondary modern — and it was housed at Darley Park and later, Breadsall. All these schools are now part of the comprehensive system and the name of Parkfields Cedars has disappeared. In addition to the state system, Derby still has a number of independent schools, the most prominent being Derby High School for Girls on Burton Road, Littleover. The city also boasts the University of Derby, when the College of Higher Education was elevated to polytechnic status just as all 'polys' became universities.

Naturally, ten centuries of education have

Top: *Bemrose School on Uttoxeter New Road, pictured when it was a boys' grammar school.* Middle: *Parkfields Cedars girls' grammar school, a name which disappeared altogether after comprehensive education was invented.* Bottom: *Genteel young Derby ladies at the School of Art in the late nineteenth century.*

produced their fair share of famous pupils. Perhaps the most illustrious of Derby's sons was John Flamsteed. Flamsteed was born at Derby in 1646. His father brought the family to Queen Street, Derby, to escape the plague and young John attended Derby School during the time of the Commonwealth.

When he was 16, Flamsteed witnessed a partial solar eclipse and it fired his imag-ination. He constructed a quadrant and measured the sun's approximate distance from each. Two years earlier, he had endured a bout of rheumatism and this forced him to leave Derby School. Nevertheless, the youth persevered with his work, eventually discovering that the old astronomical tables were inaccurate. Flamsteed went to Cam-bridge and then to London where he met

Left: *John Flamsteed, a son of Derby and the first Astronomer Royal.* Right: *Derby's Herbert Spencer, a great philosopher and the man whose plan to save the town from flooding were put successfully into operation — nearly a century later.*

Left: *Erasmus Darwin was not a Derby man but lived in the town from 1781 until his death in 1802.* Right: *Joseph Wright recorded many important Derbeians.*

Laboratory at Derby School of Science in the late nineteenth century.

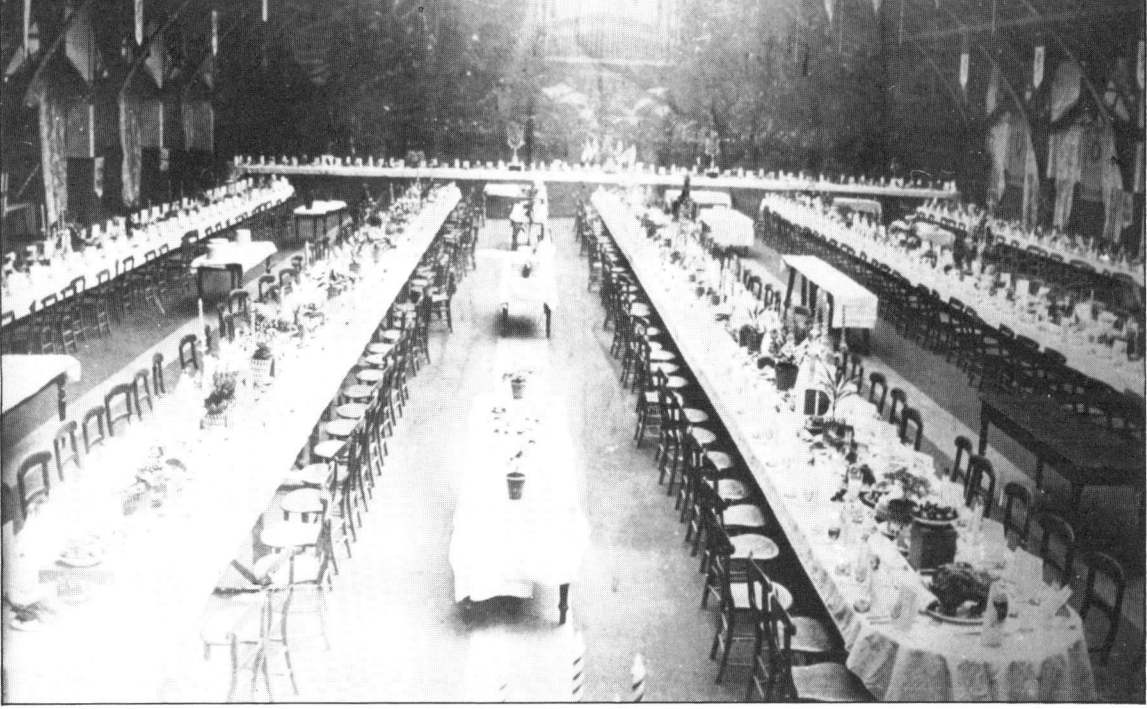

Banquet laid out in the Drill Hall in 1872 for the Prince and Princess of Wales who came to open new rooms at Derby School.

Sir Jonas Moore, Surveyor-General of Ordnance at the Tower. Moore was impressed by Derby's young genius and he evenutally became the first Astronomer Royal, fitting out the new Observatory at Greenwich. During the next 13 years, Flamsteed fixed the position of over 20,000 stars and when his father died, a legacy enabled him to obtain better equipment and therefore, greater accuracy. His contemporary, Sir Isaac Newton used much of Flamsteed's findings in his own work. Flamsteed was working on corrections and extensions of his life's work right up to his death at the age of 73.

Joseph Wright, the painter 'Wright of Derby' was also a pupil at Derby School. Born at 28 Irongate in September 1734, Wright wandered Italy before returning to his native town and St Helen's House. His pictures include landscapes and portraits, and besides many fine examples of chiaroscuro — the curious effects of strong light and deep shadows — he left several important portraits of Derby worthies. He died at 26 Queen Street on 29 August 1797 and was buried in St Alkmund's Church.

The great philosopher Herbert Spencer was a Derby man, born at 12 Exeter Row on 27 April 1820, and later moving with his family to 31 Wilmot Street, off Normanton Road. Spencer was trained as a civil engineer, contributing a report on flood prevention to Derby Town Council in 1842, before winning world fame for his works on philosophy, most of which were written in London and Brighton where he died in December 1903.

Spencer elaborated on the theory of evolution orginated by Erasmus Darwin, the grandfather of Charles Darwin. Although Erasmus was not a Derby man, he lived in the town and its immediate surrounds from 1781 until his death in 1802. One of his homes was in Full Street where he set up a doctor's practice. Erasmus Darwin married the widow of Colonel Chandos Pole and in 1784 he founded the Derby Philosophical Society. He was a member of the committee formed to bring coal into Derby via the new Erewash Canal, so that it would be sold to the poor at a low price; and he tried to pioneer free medical advice for the poor, a venture which failed at that time. Darwin did much for Derby, yet his circle of friends was small and he had the reputation of a man with exteme views who quickly offended the deep religious convictions of many of his neighbours.

One of Derby's well-known names is that of William Hutton, the historian of the town who was born in Full Street on 30 September 1723, the son of a woolcomber who liked his beer a shade too much. Hutton's autobiography gives an important insight into working class conditions in eighteenth-century Derby. Indeed, the town had many famous sons and a whole volume could be written on them alone. Samuel Richardson, the early novelist and author of *Pamela* was born in Derby. And even such relatively modern schools like Bemrose School can boast a whole host of former pupils who made good. Actors Eric Lander, James Bolam and Kevin Lloyd are just three Old Bemrosians whose names will be familiar to present-day Derbeians although the first two were not born in Derby. The city can be proud of the men and women who have passed through its schools in the past 1,000 years.

'Wayes Foule and Depe'

ERBY is a major centre of the nation's communications system, yet for centuries the roads around the town were extremely primitive. In 1585, when Mary Queen of Scots was being escorted through Derby, her gaoler, Sir Ralph Sadler, wrote: 'This day we remove this Queen to Derbie and tomorrow to Tutbury, the wayes being so foule and depe . . .that we cannot get through in a day.' One week later, Sir Ralph commented that plate and other articles might be brought on horseback from Derby much cheaper than by cart, suggesting that the trunks used should be well-lined with canvas to prevent the goods from damage as they underwent much jolting.

Nevertheless, the roads and packhorse ways in and out of Derby were comparatively busy. Pigs of lead were brought to Derby Market from Wirksworth, and the Osmaston Road was especially busy as most of Derby's exports were destined for south of the Trent. The bridge over the river at Swarkestone was under the control of the Derby Guild and as long ago as 1275, the Melbourne merchants found themselves in trouble for crossing over Swarkestone Bridge without paying tolls to Derby. The road to Nottingham took Derby goods to the Trent where they were shipped to the Humber. Yet Derby was still isolated from much of England and A.W.Davison wrote in his *Derby, Its Rise and Progress*: 'This remote situation of Derby stamped the people with an old-fashioned rusticity, long after the town had become a manufacturing centre.'

By the eighteenth century, more and more people were travelling by coach instead of

Derby's Irongate, one of the streets widened in an improvement scheme for the town centre.

Nineteenth-century
view of Derby
Market Place.

on horseback and carriers took goods and passengers in their wagons. An advertisement every Monday for the five-day journey to the Bell and Mouth Inn in London's Aldersgate, returning the following week. The roads were still bad and the wagons, drawn by six horses, had wide wheels to combat the badly-rutted highways. A fatality occurred at Mackworth when a Derby to Manchester wagoner went to sleep and fell off his wagon.

Derby was indeed a busy centre as wagons came and went to many of the major towns and cities of England, although the pack-horse was still favoured for cross country journeys north of the Trent. Daniel Defoe, writing in 1720, said that upwards of 1,000 packhorses came to Stourbridge Fair from Lancashire and Yorkshire, carrying cloth. They returned with loads of hops for Derby and other towns in the Trent Valley. Derby's inns provided for both packhorse and the horses drawing wagons, and the Angel in the Cornmarket could stable 60 horses at the end of the seventeenth century.

In 1735, the first Derby to London stage coach came into operation, leaving the George Inn every Thursday. Although a great

improvement on the carrier's wagons, the early stagecoaches were both heavy and uncomfortable, and not until the Act authorising toll gates was passed, did the roads and the coaches improve dramatically. In June 1758 a meeting of 'county gentlemen' was held at the King's Head to arrange the siting of turnpikes, or toll houses. Soon, all roads out of Derby had a gate and a tollhouse at which the keeper collected the fees. Within two decades, most of Derby's roads had been reconstructed and with that improvement came a better design of stage coach.

The old-style coach, hung on leatherstraps, gave way to coaches with steel springs. The first of these new 'flying machines', as they were called, made the journey from Derby to London in one day on 21 May 1764, although it was considered too dangerous to allow outside passengers. In 1767, the journey was cut to a then almost unbelievable ten hours, starting at the Talbot Inn at 9pm and arriving in the capital at 7am the following day.

The ever-increasing coach traffic inevitably brought more prosperity to Derby. In 1828 there were seven daily coaches to both

London and Manchester, and other services ran to Birmingham, Nottingham, Leeds and other towns. At 2am the *Independent* from Manchester to London changed horses at the Nag's Head in St Peter's Street; the *Defiance*, running the same route, changed at the Tiger Inn at 1am. Other coaches rattling through Derby included *Royal Bruce, Nelson,* and *Peveril of the Peak.* There were complaints of traffic problems, and in September 1838, Joseph Borrington was fined for driving recklessly down St Peter's Street on a Sunday morning, while a deaf man was run over by a coach in Irongate on market day.

In 1795, Derby Canal, engineered by Benjamin Outram, opened to traffic. The proposal for a canal to link with the Trent and Mersey Canal and thus connect Derby with both the North Sea and the Irish Sea, had been made two years earlier. Derby Canal was cut at a cost of £100,000, but in return for their investment in the Canal Company, local businessmen could both import and export more cheaply and more quickly. Coal, gypsum, building stone, Cornish clay and heavy iron castings from Butterley all came to the canal terminal at Derwent Wharf.

Raw cotton came into the town from the port of Liverpool and a small branch canal, known as the Phoenix Branch, was cut to rejoin the Derwent at a point just south of St Mary's Bridge. From there the river was navigable for the one and a half miles to the mill at Darley Abbey. In addition to bringing cheaper raw materials to the town and allowing Derby's own exports to reach the ports more efficiently, the Derby Canal also created new jobs at the wharf and, before long, even a bargebuilder had set up business.

There was, however, a development on the horizon which would sound the death knell of both the stage coaches and the canal barges, although it would also move Derby into a new era of unparelleled prosperity. The railway age had arrived and in August 1833 a scheme was mooted in Leicester, aimed at linking other Midland towns with the Birmingham to London railway then under construction. By November 1834, the Midland Counties Railway project planned a terminus at Derby with the proposed railway station near the present Derwent Street, crossing the river near today's Exeter Bridge. Other schemes were being hatched in October 1835; a proposed Derby to Birmingham railway was being considered, as well as a North Midland line between Derby and Leeds.

The battle between the rival railway companies was joined and the *Derby Mercury* considered that the scheme would 'make Derby a centre of communications and must, we imagine, increase the trade and importance of the town'. Never has a local

Left: *Derby Railway Station in 1842, on the threshhold of a new era for the town.* Right: *Another early view of the town's main railway station, in the 1870s.*

Goods train enters Derby Midland Station in the 1950s.

newspaper printed more prophetic words. The North Midland's terminus was to be at Nottingham Road and the Derby and Birmingham Company decided to continue their line across the Derwent to join up to the North Midland property as a means of establishing through communications. In December 1835, Derby's Mayor, Richard Wright Haden chaired a big public meeting at which the two companies' plans were given wide approval. Two months later Derby Town Council suggested that a joint station for all three companies should be built on the Holmes, proposing that Thorntree Lane be widened and the brook between St James' Lane and St Peter's Street be covered to form a road from the town centre to the station.

Although the Derby and Birmingham company agreed in principle, the Midland Counties and the North Midland objected on the grounds that the site was liable to flooding. Eventually, the nearest high ground in Castlefields was selected, though not before the Midland Counties attempted

to alter its route to by-pass Derby — and the competition for London traffic — altogether.

A petition protesting against this was signed by over 2,000 Derby people in less than 24 hours, and by June 1838 the three companies had agreed to a trijunct station. In March the following year, plans were published for the new terminus at Derby.

On Thursday, 30 May 1839, the Midland Counties Railway opened its Derby to Nottingham line and the company's three engines — *Sunbeam*, *Ariel* and *Hawk* — brought 500 people to a temporary platform at Derby Junction. Four days later, the regular service began with four trains daily in each direction, and two on Sundays. The following August, the Derby to Birmingham line was opened and Derbeians could now reach London in six and three-quarter hours. The Midland Counties had used 4,035 'navvies' and 57 horses in constructing their line, but the North Midland faced greater problems with many tunnels and bridges between Derby and Leeds and it was some time before that line was opened.

Derby's 'Great Central Railway Station', designed by Francis Thompson, was opened in 1840 and although it has been altered considerably, the original design for the three separate companies still dictates the layout of the present station at the end of Midland Road. In 1980, the Victorian frontage

of the station still existed, together with the musty old corridors of the former glory days, including the once splendid Board Room of the Midland Railway Company — a result of a merger between the three original companies operating from Derby. British Rail had a £3-million plan to completely rebuild the station to which the City Council agreed although local organisations were deeply divided over the issue. Eventually it came to pass.

But in the mid-nineteenth century, almost everyone agreed that the station was a wonder to behold. Within a year of its opening, Derby saw its first day-trippers when Sheffield people paid four shillings return each to come to Derby and see the station and the nearby Arboretum. More lines opened and soon Derby was connected to almost every important town and city in the country.

It was also a fortunate day for Derby when the newly-formed Midland Railway Company decided to make its home at Derby. Derby Locomotive Works had opened in 1840 to service and maintain the engines of the Midland Counties and North Midlands companies. When the Midland Railway opened its Carriage and Wagon Works in 1873, Derby was set to become the centre of the nation's railway engineering industry. The railways did not come a moment too soon for Derby as the old silk-throwing and

Derby Railway Station after modernisation had swept away the Victorian façade.

stocking-weaving trades began to decline rapidly.

Yet 3 November 1855, was a sad day as William Burditt drove the last Manchester to Derby coach into the town. It rattled down

Derby Corporation electric tram pictured in 1904.

Sadler Gate and groaned into the Bell Inn Yard, disappearing from Derby's story. The canal, too was in decline and although its official closure was not announced until as recently as 2 February 1970, it had been virtually redundant since 1935.

The effect of the railway on Derby was enormous, for besides becoming the biggest employer of labour in the town, which itself created the need for more housing, particularly in the Litchurch area, it created new markets for Derby's goods, enabled raw materials to be imported even more cheaply and quickly, and enabled Derby's shoppers to reach new markets. This in turn made the town's shopkeepers, who had hitherto enjoyed a monopoly, look to their prices and service.

The railway also encouraged local road travel and in the earliest days, Derby's principal coach proprietor, W. W. Wallis, was appointed agent for the Derby and Birmingham, and Midland Counties companies, running a service between the town centre and the station. It was Derby's first local bus service. Until 1880, independent operators ran the local transport services, but the Derby

Derby Corporation trolley bus outside the Midland Station. These electrically-powered buses ran from the 1930s until the late 1960s.

Tramways Order of 1879 gave the Derby Tramways Company powers to buy out the private operators and run its own tramway and omnibus system. Horse-drawn trams ran up Ashbourne, London, Osmaston and Normanton Roads for a universal fare of twopence, later reduced to one penny.

On 1 November 1899, the company was taken over by the Corporation and the Derby Corporation Act of 1901 gave the council powers to build up to 17½ miles of tramway route, including the reconstruction of existing lines, for mechanical traction. Soon, Derby had its overhead electric tramway system and by 1909, it had almost reached what would be its ultimate size of some 14 miles. The development of the motor bus service was slow, but in 1929 it was obvious that the tramway system, which had been allowed to deteriorate badly during World

Flood in the Cornmarket in May 1932. This was the last time that the town was inundated by Markeaton Brook. A flood prevention scheme, first mooted by Herbert Spencer almost a century earlier, was then put into operation.

*Derby Canal at the
Siddals in 1874,
showing lock and
lock-keeper's house.*

*Left: The old
wooden Long Bridge
which carried the
canal towpath over
the Derwent. It was
demolished in the
1950s. Right: Work
is under way to
widen Exeter Bridge
in 1930.*

*Markeaton Brook
flows under
Victoria Street. This
photograph was take
in the early 1950s.*

War One, was reaching the end of its life. In 1932 Derby's first trolley bus service opened and by 1935 the changeover was complete. The trolley bus was a familiar sight in Derby — with its infuriating habit of becoming disconnected from the overhead wires — until the 1960s when the last trolley bus ran down Normanton Road and Derby's bus service became totally motorised.

The roads and streets of Derby which Sir Ralph Sadler found 'so foule and depe' have presented problems to successive local administrations until fairly recent times, due to the consistent flooding of Markeaton Brook. The first recorded flood was in 1587 and throughout the seventeenth and eighteenth centuries, the town centre found itself inundated. On Friday, 1 April 1842, some £30,000 worth of damage was done as the water burst open shop doors, ruining goods. The *Derby Mercury* published a table of measurements taken at the height of the deluge and this recorded that the water had reached a depth of 6ft in the Cornmarket, 5ft in Sadler Gate and Becket Well Lane, and over 3ft in Cheapside, Friar Gate and Tenant Street, to name but a few parts of the town centre under water. In 1932, the brook flooded again following heavy rain and people travelled Derby's streets by boat. At last the Council carried out a scheme to divert the brook. It was a scheme very similar to that which Herbert Spencer had suggested one hundred years earlier. At last the streets of Derby were freed from the dangers which had threatened them for centuries.

Town of Trade

IN 1720, Daniel Defoe passed through Derby and recorded that it was a town 'of gentry rather than of trade'. How all that was to change within the course of the next few years. The vision and flair of a small number of men was to change Derby from a relatively modest market town to a centre of manufacture with mills and factories which would attract trade and visitors from near and far.

A survey of 1693 showed that Derby had 694 dwelling houses, 76 malthouses and 120 ale houses. The demands of the town on Derby's existing wells and springs was great and it had long been apparent that a new system of feeding water to the town had to be found. The man who devised the system which gave Derby its first proper water supply was a millwright and engineer, George Sorocold. In the early 1690s, Sorocold built a floating water-wheel on the Derwent near St Alkmund's Mills. The wheel pumped water into a reservoir at St Michael's Church, where it was pumped to 'King Streete, Irongate, Market Place, Rotton Roe, and the Corn Market in Derby and so to the Gaole Bridge in the said Borough' through pipes bored out of elm trunks.

Water power was to play a great part in Derby's early industrial development and at the beginning of the eighteenth century, just after Sorocold's water supply scheme had begun its operations, the stocking industry came to Derby. Over a century earlier, an obscure Nottingham clergyman had invented the first hand-worked stocking machines which were operated at home by the stockinger and his children. The trade had been established in Derby for only a short while when Thomas Cotchett, an elderly barrister born at Mickleover before the Civil War, introduced Dutch silk machines to the town. When Cotchett needed an experienced millwright to install his machines in the mill he had built on an islet in the Derwent, he turned to Sorocold.

Derby Silk Mill, built in 1717 and probably the first factory in England. The building was destroyed by fire in 1910 and now only the tower survives.

But Cotchett's venture was doomed to failure, due to lack of capital and enterprise, and it was one of his apprentices, John Lombe, who made a success of establishing a silk mill. Lombe had heard that Italian machines were far superior to the Dutch ones and he set off for Italy where he obtained a job in a mill at Piedmont. Lombe indulged in an early form of industrial espionage and secretly copied down details of the machines before slipping back to England in 1717. With capital supplied by his half-brother, Thomas, Lombe built a five-storey mill next to Cotchett's doomed venture and with Sorocold's help, installed the Italian-style machines.

Derby's silk mill can lay claim to be England's first real factory and it brought

The Silk Mill Gates made by Robert Bakewell are visible in this photograph.

Left: *Derby Silk Mill workers from an engraving of 1843.* Right: *George Sorocold's water-engine house of about 1765.*

Left: *Derby Borough Fire Brigade pour water on the Silk Mill during the disastrous fire of 1910.* Right (upper): *Spa Lane Mills, the home of Ernest Turner (Dould) Ltd, pictured in the 1950s.* Right (lower): *Derby Power Station, Sowter Road. Now demolished.*

much-needed work and prosperity to eighteenth-century Derby. Although conditions were hard — William Hutton tells of working there at the age of seven and being caned for idleness — the wages were by no means poor in comparison to the average income of a working class Derby man of the time. The story of John Lombe has several romantic twists and when he died in 1722, aged just 29, it was rumoured that he had been poisoned by a beautiful woman, sent by the Italians who were angry at his subterfuge. Lombe was given a great public funeral by the grateful people of Derby before being laid to rest in All Saints'.

Thomas Lombe became the sole owner of the mill and he was eventually knighted and given £14,000 for his services to the country. The original mill partly collapsed in 1891 and was demolished, being replaced by a new building which itself was destroyed by fire in 1910. The only remains of the original

Left: *The pioneering Jedidiah Strutt, who developed the 'Derby Rib' stocking frame.* Right: *The old Nottingham Road china factory illustrated in 1756.*

Left: *John Heath, banker, twice Mayor of Derby and founder of the pot work on Cockpit Hill, where William Duesbury came to work. This portrait of Heath was painted by Joseph Wright.* Right: *Pattern gilding at the Royal Crown Derby works on Osmaston Road.*

mill are the magnificent Silk Mill Gates, executed by Robert Bakewell and at the time of writing, standing next to the Museum and Art Gallery in the Wardwick, although there is a plan to remove them to their original site.

When Jedidiah Strutt married into a family of hosiers, it paved the way for the famous 'Derby ribbed frame'. Strutt's brother-in-law, William Woollatt talked of the advantages enjoyed by a machine which would automatically produce ribbed hose. Strutt began work on just such a machine and eventually produced one which, when attached to a conventional stocking frame, would regulate it to produce the required pattern. Strutt and Woollatt enjoyed the monopoly of the invention until the patent expired in 1773. Two years earlier, Strutt had gone into partnership with Richard Arkwright, inventor of a cotton-spinning machine. Arkwright was working his machine by a horse-turned wheel in Nottingham when he heard of Lombe's water-driven mill. With financial help from Strutt, Arkwright opened a water-powered mill at Cromford. Strutt, too, opened factories at Milford, Belper and Derby, where the first all-cotton cloth in

England was woven. The Tenant Street factory was England's first fire-proof factory, with floors of hollow brick, and for a while the future of the cotton industry lay between Derby and Manchester until Brindley's canal settled the matter in Lancashire's favour. Derby's canal was still some two decades away.

The first half of the eighteenth century also saw the birth of the china works which was to make the name of Derby world-famous. About 1750, Alderman John Heath — a banker and twice Mayor of Derby — opened a pot works on Cockpit Hill. Heath needed craftsmen of the highest calibre and William Duesbury, an artist and enameller at the famous Chelsea works, came to Derby where he worked with Heath and with a French refugee called Andrew Planche who had a small works in Lodge Lane. In 1769, Duesbury and Heath were able to buy the Chelsea Works and four years later, George III gave them permission to mark Derby china with a crown, thus giving birth to Crown Derby. In 1776, the china factory at

Bow was also acquired and when Heath went bankrupt in 1780, Duesbury worked the three factories alone before amalgamating them in 1784 and moving the entire operation to Derby.

Duesbury died in 1786, to be succeeded by his son, also named William. Duesbury junior found the business too much of a burden and took a partner in Michael Kean, a London miniature painter. When the second Duesbury died, Kean married his widow; and when her son, the third William Duesbury showed no inclination to go into the family business, the reign of the Duesburys came to an abrupt end. In 1809, Robert Bloor, a salesman under Duesbury and Kean, bought the business and by 1832 it had grown from a 70-strong workforce in 1790, to over 180.

Bloor was now suffering from ill-health and the factory was put in charge of a manager whose ability did not match his ambition. Bloor died in 1846 and three years later, Crown Derby works closed down. The best of the moulds and models, together with

Left: *Silhouette of William Duesbury.* Right: *John Whitehurst, a fine clockmaker who enjoyed a 40-year association with Derby.*

the pattern books and the rights to use various marks, were disposed of to a group of leading potters and artists who continued the production of Derby china in a new factory in King Street. In 1877, a new company was formed and this proved to be the lifeline for Derby china. Big markets were opened up in Canada and the United States, and in 1890, Queen Victoria granted the Derby Crown Porcelain Company a Royal Warrant of Appointment. Royal Crown Derby was born and the company, now established in Osmaston Road, was to earn lasting fame in the story of the city.

Derby might, however, have turned away one famous craftsman who brought his talent to the town. In 1735, John Whitehurst, a clockmaker from Congleton in Cheshire, came to Derby to open a shop, only to be told that as he was not a freeman, he would be unable to start a business in the town. Whitehurst struck a compromise by mending the Guildhall clock free of charge and began a 40-year association with the town which so nearly denied itself his skill and expertise.

In 1809, the Shot Tower was built in the Morledge. Molten lead was poured through sieves at the top, forming tiny drops which were rounded off as they spun through the air.

For over a century the tower was one of Derby's best known landmarks and although it was demolished in 1931, its name lives on to describe that area of the city on the corner of Albert Street and the Morledge.

The industrial history of Derby has been relatively peaceful, but in 1833, the town saw the celebrated 'Derby Turnout' when hundreds of newly-joined trades unionists found themselves locked out because of their membership of the Grand National Consolidated Trade Union. Weavers, silk-throwers, knitters and builders — in fact, all kinds of Derby workmen and women — joined the union, and in November 1833, Mr Frost, a silk manufacturer, sacked a man who refused to pay a fine for bad workmanship. Eight hundred workers went on strike in support of their colleague and when other mill workers joined in, the employers retaliated by refusing to employ any union members.

By 4 December, 1,300 workers were out; by February, the number had swollen to over 2,000, while the owners kept the mills running with unskilled non-union labour. Derby saw its first pickets and two women

were arrested for allegedly insulting women workers, while Thomas Mead was given three months' imprisonment for trying to persuade Walter Wood, a journeyman, to join the strike. Dragoons and special constables were drafted in to keep order, and the strike dragged on. By March, the strike pay of seven shillings per man had run out, and strikers began to drift back to work. On Monday, 21 April 1834, the final strikers asked to be reinstated, although over 600 found that their services were no longer required.

Much of this news was carried in the *Derby Mercury* which was founded in 1732, the year following the closure of Derby's first local newspaper, the *Derby Postman*, first published in 1717. The *Derby Journal* (ceased 1780) was perhaps a more campaigning newspaper than the *Mercury*, and in 1823, the *Derby and Chesterfield Reporter* began publication as the organ of the Reform Party. Newspaper Stamp Duty put the cost of newspapers beyond most working people and Henry Robinson was fined £20 for selling unstamped newspapers in Derby Market Place. Unable to pay the fine, Robinson was sentenced to six months' imprisonment but the Home Secretary of the day soon released him. The *Reporter* ceased publication in 1931 and the *Mercury* in 1930. The *Derbyshire*

Advertiser was published from 1846 to 1976 — most of that time from its Market Place office — and the *Derby Daily Express* from 1885 to 1932 when it was taken over by the *Derby Daily Telegraph* (founded in 1879), a merger which ended the local circulation war and which gave birth to the present *Derby Evening Telegraph* title.

Perhaps the most famous name associated with Derby's industrial story is that of Rolls-Royce Limited. In 1906, the company decided to build its new headquarters in the town at Osmaston Road, and that faith has been repaid by the fine workmanship of thousands of Derby men and women over the last 75 years. Although Royce's reputation was made with its cars, the motor car side of the business eventually went to Crewe and Derby became the centre of the aero-engine division.

The first aero-engine was produced during World War One and called *Eagle*. Alcock and Brown's historic transatlantic flight in 1918 was powered by an *Eagle VIII*, and the 1929 and 1931 Schneider Trophy races were won by 'planes powered by the 'R' engine. There followed the *Falcon, Kestrel, Buzzard* and, of course, the *Merlin*, synonymous with the Spitfires and Hurricanes of the Battle of Britain in 1940. Since the last war, the *Welland, Dart, Derwent* and *Nene* 'River

Market Hall interior pictured in 1866.

Shops in St Peter's Street just after World War One. Some seventy years later the street was pedestrianised as part of the Derby Promenade scheme which banned traffice along the old north-south trackway from Irongate to The Spot.

Class' engines have all come out of the Derby works, as too, has the RB211 on which the future prosperity of Rolls-Royce depended so much, especially after the 'crash' of 1971.

It is difficult to know where to draw the line when speaking of the many famous names of Derby industry. Over the years, firms like Qualcast, International Combustion, Aiton's, Brown's Foundry, E.W.Bliss, British Celanese, Fletcher and Stewarts, Bemrose, Spiral Tube and many more, have all made Derby respected throughout the world as a manufacturing centre with a reputation for quality and service. Some have even added a dash of colour to the city as in Siddals Road where until the early 1980s ICI's works left the pavements a rainbow of colours and where bright green, yellow and blue-coloured workmen once crossed and re-crossed the road, to the astonishment of newcomers just arrived at the nearby railway station.

Many family firms are also remembered for their contribution to the shopping needs of Derby people; and in 1850 the first Co-

An RB211-524 fan jet aero engine. This is a later development of the engine which led to the crash of the firm in 1971 but air passengers all over the world are still transported by Derby-made engines.

operative store was opened in the George Yard in Sadler Gate. Jonathan Henderson of the Carpenters' and Joiners' Union was the first president and secretary of a movement which had just £2 capital when it was founded. In 1858 the Co-op transferred its premises to a warehouse in Biggs Yard, Victoria Street, and two years later opened its membership to the general public. It never looked back, with its bakery, works department, transport department, dairy and even its own abattoir and pork factory making it one of the most diverse co-operatives in the country. Eventually, centralisation saw it absorbed into a larger regional society — the Central Midlands Co-op — and much of the industry centred on Derby, like the bakery, disappeared.

The Pursuit of Leisure

THE inhabitants of Derby have always looked for ways of putting their leisure time to good use, although many of the pastimes practised in the town over the centuries would hardly qualify for the description of sport as we know it today. Wrestling was one Saxon pastime we still find acceptable in the twentieth century, but the Saxons also indulged in such barbaric activities as badger-baiting and cock-fighting. Indeed, it was not until the early part of the last century that these 'pleasures' were finally stamped out.

An Elizabethan cockpit stood in Cockpit Hill, and early in the seventeenth century, during the reign of James I, a new cockpit was built on Nun's Green. In 1738 the 'Gentlemen' of Derbyshire and Staffordshire staged what amounted to an inter-county cock-fighting match at the Old Swan in St Peter's Parish when 31 birds tore each other to pieces; and in 1772, spectators crowded the Market Place to watch a bull being baited.

Horse racing was an ever popular sport in Derby and until 1803 the races took place on Sinfin Moor, with all the accompanying hubbub of sideshows, cock-fighting and concerts. When the moor was enclosed, a new racecourse was laid out on The Holmes, although local landowners objected to this, and in 1845, as more and more open land was swallowed up by industry, the races moved again, this time to the Nottingham Road area which is still known as The Racecourse.

For 90 years, Derby Racecourse attracted some of the greatest names in the world of horse racing. In 1921, for instance, Steve Donoghue won the £1,900 Peveril of the Peak Plate on J.B. Joel's *Corn Sack* during the Derby Summer Meeting; and in August 1939, in the last meeting before World War Two, Gordon Richards rode at Derby. It was, in fact, the last-ever meeting here. When peace was restored, Derby Town Council decided that horse racing brought too many 'undesirables' to the town and the venue, which had been used by the Army during the war, was never re-opened as a race track and was laid out with football pitches by the parks department.

That in itself was slightly ironic, for the Nottingham Road ground was the original home of Derby County until they moved to the Baseball Ground in 1895. The Rams were formed as an off-shoot of Derbyshire County Cricket Club and few people realise that an FA Cup Final replay was once played at Derby. Nottingham Road had seen several important soccer games following the Rams' formation in 1884 and several Cup semi-finals were played there. In 1886, Blackburn Rovers drew 0-0 with West Bromwich Albion in the FA Cup Final at Kennington Oval and the replay was staged at Derby where Blackburn won 2-0 to take the trophy for the third consecutive year.

On 8 September 1888, the Rams played their first game as founder-members of the Football League when they met Bolton Wanderers at Pike's Lane, Bolton. The Trotters were 3-0 ahead after only six minutes, but Derby fought back to win 6-3, eventually having to apply for re-election after finishing the season in the bottom four. Derby County played in two successive FA Cup Finals, in 1898 and 1899, losing to Nottingham Forest and Sheffield United respectively at The Crystal Palace. The Rams were back in the Final of 1903, losing 6-0 to Bury, a record that still stands. Derby fans

Above: *South Derbyshire meet the touring Australian Aboriginals at Derby in 1868.* Opposite: *Derbyshire CCC bazaar at the Drill Hall in 1902. As always the club were desperate to raise money. The theme was 'Olde Derby'.*

had to wait until 1946 for the FA Cup to come to Derby for the first, and so far, only time when the Rams beat Charlton Athletic 4-1 in the first post-war Wembley Cup Final.

Derby had to wait even longer for their first League Championship. Brian Clough, who rescued the club from the doldrums of the 1950s and 1960s, brought the title to the Baseball Ground in 1972. Controversy has never been far away from the club and in October 1973, Clough sensationally left Derby. Another title was added in 1975 but the club was on the verge of decline and at the end of the 1979-80 season, the Rams were relegated to the Second Division. Since then they have been down to the Third, back up to the First, and then down again to the Second Division, which is now perversely

The Derby Racecourse stand in 1859.

An engraving of 1859 showing the races at Nottingham Road.

named the 'First' because the top division split off to become the so-called Premier League.

Controversy still dogged the club — they nearly went out of business in their Centenary Year — and Robert Maxwell, later to be dubbed 'the world's biggest swindler' took over. Eventually, his shadow was removed and the club was bought by Lionel Pickering, a local man who had made his millions with the free newspaper Trader Group.

Derby County, through legendary names like Steve Bloomer, Jack Barker, Sammy Crooks, Raich Carter, Peter Doherty and more recently, Roy McFarland, is part of football's rich story. No doubt the club will rise again, especially given that it is now in caring local ownership once more.

Derbyshire County Cricket Club was born in 1870, following a meeting at the Guildhall in November that year. Cricket had been played in the town for a number of years

Derby County pictured in 1949-50. The Rams were then a First Division force. Back row (left to right): Jack Poole (trainer), Tim Ward, Bert Mozley, Terry Webster, Leon Leuty, Chick Musson and Jack Howe. Front row: Reg Harrison, Johnny Morris, Jack Stamps, Billy Steel, Frank Broome.

with the South Derbyshire CC as the main club, playing on the Holmes before moving to Nottingham Road in 1863. On 2 and 3 September 1868, South Derbyshire beat a team of Australian Aboriginals by 139 runs at Derby. The colourful tourists included such players as Dick-a-Dick, Red Cap, Two Penny and Mosquito, and at the end of play they treated the spectators to a display of boomerang throwing.

Derbyshire CCC's first county match was at Manchester in May 1871 when they beat Lancashire by 62 runs with Unwin Sowter scoring 47 not out. Although Derbyshire are sometimes listed as County Champions for 1874, this was under a highly unsatisfactory 'least lost' rule and the club's only proper title came in 1936 when Derbyshire pipped Middlesex and Yorkshire, thanks to the sterling efforts of such great cricketers as Denis Smith, Stan Worthington, Bill Copson, Charlie Elliott, Tommy Mitchell and Leslie Townsend. In the early 1980s, Derbyshire cricket enjoyed something of a revival

and the county had three players — Mike Hendrick, Bob Taylor and Geoff Miller — playing in the same 1979 England team. In 1981 they won the NatWest Trophy.

More recently, under the captaincy of Kim Barnett, Derbyshire were the Sunday League champions and have finished high in the County Championship. The County Ground at Nottingham Road, for so long an embarrassing venue with hardly any of the facilities associated with a major professional sports ground, has been developed and is now as pleasant as most English cricket grounds. Further developments are planned, although the club is still desperately short of money.

Professional boxing also had a great following in Derby, especially just before and just after World War Two, and on the amateur scene Derby Borough Police Boxing Club was considered to be one of the best in the country. Open-air tournaments were held on the Municipal Sports Ground and, during the war, at the Baseball Ground. The King's Hall was a popular venue right up to the early 1960s when professional boxing went into a nationwide decline and the number of licensed fighters diminished rapidly.

Derby Rowing Club and Derby and County Athletic Club each have long and honourable histories dating back to the last century. The rowing club is over 100 years old and the athletic club celebrated its centenary in 1985. Both have sent performers to all the major international events over the years and Derby men and women have competed in the Olympic Games. Arthur Keilly ran in the 1960 Rome Olympics marathon and, most recently, Derby's Fiona May represented Great Britain in the Barcelona Olympics, although she was injured in the very early stages of the long-jump competition.

The Derbyshire Football Association was founded in 1883 and has administered the game for local amateur and semi-professional players, governing the wide range of leagues within Derby. In 1964, Sunday footballers were allowed the right to join the ranks of the DFA.

But the story of Derby's leisure is not confined to sport; more cultural pursuits have also occupied citizens. After years of bands of strolling players setting up booths in inn yards, theatrical performances were occasionally held in the very first Assembly Rooms in Full Street. These Assembly Rooms, built in 1714, were eventually replaced by a much grander building in the Market Place, opened in 1765. The second Assembly Rooms was the scene for eighteenth-century Derby's social whirl, and concerts, balls and dinners were held under a fine ceiling and magnificent chandelier. The only shopkeeper allowed to attend the 'Assemblies' was one Henry Franceys, a local apothecary and a great favourite with the gentry.

Generations of Derby dancers from all walks of life eventually used the Assembly Rooms and for a time it housed the offices of the Derby Savings Bank, as well as serving the town as a recruiting office in 1939. It was gutted by fire in 1963, but it had played such an important part in the story of Derby, that it was no surprise when the City Council

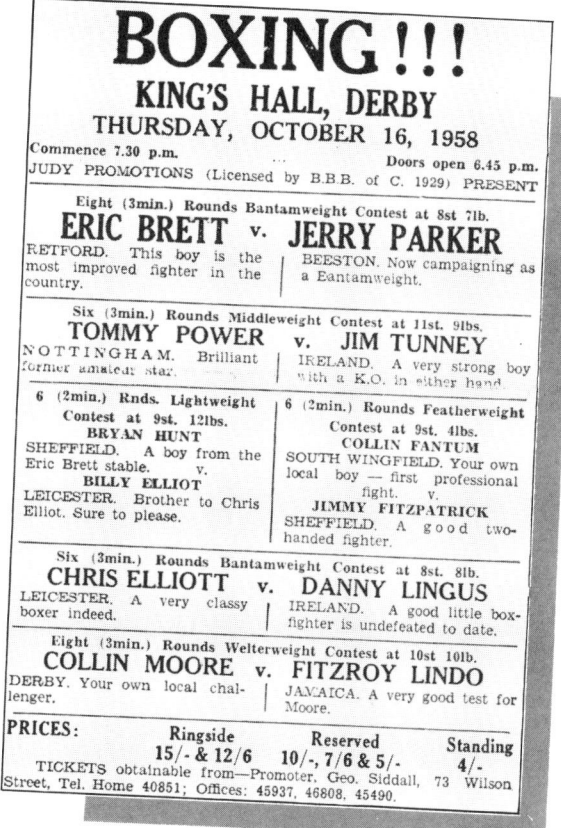

retained the name for their civic complex, which was opened in the Market Place by the Queen Mother on 9 November 1977.

Although theatrical productions were staged at various venues before 1773 — including a room in Irongate — September of that year marked the opening of Derby's first true theatre in Bold Lane, with Goldsmith's new comedy *She Stoops to Conquer*. It ceased to be a theatre in 1864 after staging a wide variety of productions from Shakespeare's *Richard III*, to one Mr Matthews 'at home for positively one night only', entertaining the audience with a monologue entitled *Trip to Paris*. Many great names of the English stage came to Bold Lane, including Edmund Kean. The great violinist Paganini also played there.

The Grand Theatre in Babington Lane (now Ritzy's) opened in 1886 and survived a serious fire to bring Derby such famous names as Sir Harry Lauder, Sybil Thorndike and, during the 1920s, the London Players with Raymond Francis. The Hippodrome in Green Lane (now inevitably a bingo hall) opened its doors for the first time just before World War One. Although it became a cinema for a time, its name was synonymous

with the best light entertainers in show-business; it is said that Flanagan and Allen wrote *Underneath the Arches* while appearing at Derby Hippodrome and the large houses in Crompton Street and Wilson Street took in 'theatricals', with the Queen's Hotel in Crompton Street as the favourite watering hole of the stars.

Derby shared in the golden era of the music-hall and Northcliffe House, former home of the *Derby Evening Telegraph*, was originally the Corn Exchange before becoming the Palace Theatre of Varieties. Even as a Corn Exchange the building saw some of the great names, including Jenny Lind, 'The Swedish Nightingale', and Sims Reeves. Opened in 1862, it filled the void between the closing of the Bold Lane theatre and the opening of the Grand. When the threatre in Babington Lane opened, the old Corn Exchange declined, despite appearances by Dan Leno and Marie Lloyd. Eventually, T.Allan Edwardes took it over and his reign, during which it was renamed the Palace, saw it take on a new lease of life with twice-nightly performances, from melodrama to light entertainment.

The fortunes of the Palace and the Grand were reversed and in 1904, F.W.Purcell sold his Grand Theatre to T.Allan Edwardes, who ran them both until 1916. Charlie Chaplin is supposed to have appeared at the Palace but local theatrical historian Harry Greatorex disputed this. He said that although Charlie Chaplin did appear with his father's clog dancing act, it would have been Chaplin senior who was at Derby. After World War One, the Palace became the Palais de Danse, with a local syndicate operating dances every night and a tea dance on Wednesday afternoons. But times were hard and in 1929 and first newspaper press roared into action in the vastly altered interior.

The late 1920s also saw the sad end of another place of entertainment when the Concert Party Pavilion at the Cavendish — home of the 'Super Optimists' — burned down. The cinema, which came to Derby in the years preceding World War One with the Picture House in Green Lane, was gaining in popularity and in the post-World War Two period, there were a score of cinemas in and around the immediate Derby area, and large queues each night for 'the pictures'. Here, as elsewhere, television killed off the great cinema era, just as the cinemas

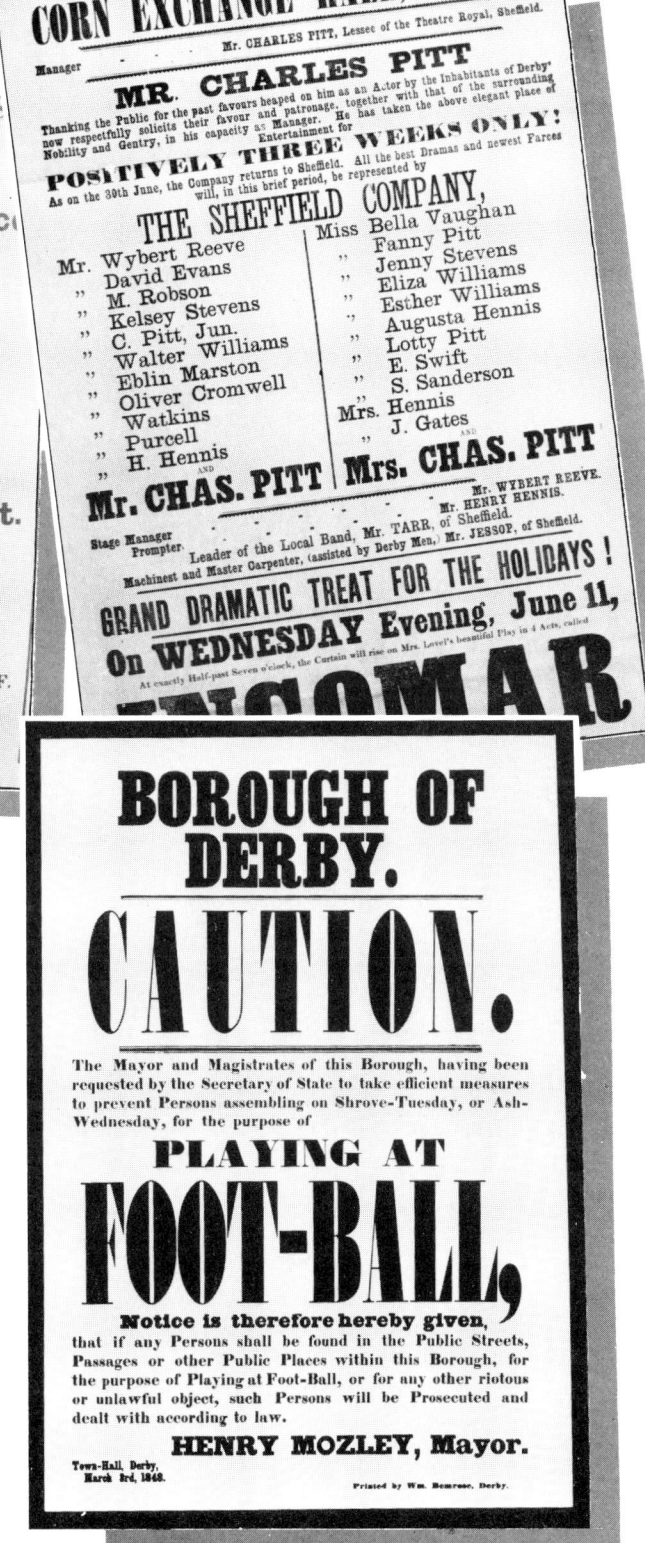

themselves had sounded the death knell for the music hall, and in 1980 Derby city centre had only two, multi-screen, cinemas — the Odeon, formerly the Gaumont on London Road, and the ABC, formerly the Regal in East Street. Even they closed down but cinema-goers are now well catered for with two multiplex cinemas — the Showcase and the UCI — and the Metro, a sort of cinema club in Green Lane.

Repertory theatre has been well supported over the years. The Little Theatre in Becket Street, opened just after the war, eventually gave way to the Derby Playhouse in Sacheverel Street. The Playhouse survived a major fire to rise up like the phoenix which now adorns the new Playhouse building in the Eagle Centre. And Derby's citizens have never been content to simply pay and watch: the city boasts many excellent amateur dramatic and operatic societies. In addition, small privately owned art galleries in Green Lane and Irongate serve to enrich the culture of the city.

Derby has also enjoyed the attentions of several benefactors. Michael Bass gave the town a museum in 1876 — the Gothic-style building with a Franco-Flemish central

tower was designed by R.K.Freeman — and he also presented The Holmes as a recreation ground which became known to thousands of Derby children as simply 'Bass's Rec'. Derby has also had a reputation for fine parks and open spaces and it is only fitting that it should boast England's first public park.

Joseph Strutt gave the Arboretum to the

Proud mother and daughter photographed by the boar statue in Derby Arborteum around 1925.

town in 1840. It was designed by John Claudius Loudon, who gave his name to a nearby street, and although it has seen grander days, it is still a pleasant oasis in a heavily built-up area. Derby has been acquiring open spaces ever since and the pre-war parks of Markeaton and Darley have been joined by the rolling acres of Elvaston and Allestree, in addition to dozens of recreation grounds and allotments. Even the traffic islands in Derby have always had a reputation for their horticulture, although in these days of public-spending cuts the better ones rely on private sponsorship.

Old Town, New City

DERBY entered the 1980s as Britain's newest city. The honour, for so long sought by a succession of local administrations, was finally accorded during the Queen's Silver Jubilee celebrations of 1977 and although Derby still waits to be told that its chief citizen may be styled Lord Mayor, the combination of the Jubilee and the city charter gave Derbeians an excuse to indulge in a wealth of street parties and bunting on a scale not seen since the Coronation of 1953.

Ever since 1927 there have been people who argued that Derby ought to be a city, simply because it is the home of a cathedral — or even because it had a 'City Hospital'. That viewpoint is to do it a great disservice, by ignoring the immense contribution which Derby has made towards the rich fabric of the British nation. We have already recorded the great steps in the city's story, and paid tribute to the sons and daughters of Derby who, in times of war and peace, gave so much to the country. But what of Derby today?

It has often been a criticism of Derby's planners and councillors that they have lagged behind their contemporaries. If the criticism is fair, then in many ways it has worked in Derby's favour. When many towns and cities were hurling up great tower blocks — hailing them as the great panacea to the nation's housing problems — Derby did not. And now the problems of high-rise living have been exposed, Derby is fortunate in having few examples of this particular twentieth-century folly.

Thanks partly to this, and partly to the fact that Derby did not suffer saturation bombing during World War Two, the city has comparatively little of the glass and concrete so characteristic of other Midland boroughs. This is not to say, however, that Derby has escaped the short-sightedness of some administrations and for over a century, much of the evidence of Derby's historic past has been steadily destroyed. Only comparatively recently has the preservation of our heritage become important enough to define certain parts of Derby as conservation areas, thanks in no small part to organisations like Derby Civic Society.

What has gone cannot be replaced, however. Stevens' Victorian church of St Alkmund has disappeared and cars and lorries now roar over the site of one of England's most romantic shrines — a site with direct connections with the turmoil of early England — and building the by-pass, the planners also destroyed a beautiful Georgian square in St Alkmund's Churchyard; the Victorians drove Becket Street through one end of the splendid Jacobean House; they also demolished Exeter House in Full Street where Bonnie Prince Charlie's 1745 rebellion came to an end; one of Derby's most picturesque antiquities, the magnificent Tudor timbered Old Mayor's Parlour in the Tenant Street area, was allowed to decay until it was necessary to demolish it in January 1948 and the area is now a gaping water-logged hole awaiting an hotel development which has been aborted more than once; and since the war, also, the mansions at Markeaton Park and Darley Park have been wiped off the face of Derby's earth.

One of the most pleasant views in Derby until relatively recently was that which looked up East Street — formerly Bag Lane — towards the church of St Peter. Now a commercial access bridge has been thrown across the roadway, blocking out the church and creating an effect which jars the eye.

Aerial view of Derby in 1928 showing the Cattle Market, Cox's Lead Works, the Long Bridge, Exeter Bridge and the Power Station. There is no Council House yet on the west bank.

Junction of Green Lane, Babington Lane, Burton Road and Normanton Road photographed before World War One.

Abbott's Hill House, Babington Lane, showing the nineteenth-century gates in Degge Street. The house was demolished in 1926.

Equally, the planners could have used the new Derby Playhouse to enhance what has always been a fairly bleak part of the city. Instead, the Playhouse presents its uninspiring rear to that part of the inner ring road near Traffic Street, looking for all the world like some fire station.

Yet there are signs that Derby is now getting it right. Georgian Friar Gate, Derby's most beautiful approach, has been preserved to the extent that No 46 — the last private residence in Friar Gate — has been absorbed into a modern office block, but only after the Georgian façade was maintained in harmony with the rest of this noble street. And in No 41, once the home of architect Joseph Pickford, there is now the city's Pickford House Museum, offering a snapshot of eighteenth-century Derby life.

Ancient Derby was compacted around the confluence of the Derwent and Markeaton Brook, and for those who know where to look, there is still plenty of evidence of the city's origins; it is still possible to take a stroll and understand just how Derby was developed from Saxon settlement, through Danish Borough, to its present status as a major industrial city, yet one which still

Demolished: Left: *The Green Man Inn, St Peter's Church-yard, pictured in 1874.* Right: *St Alk-mund's Church and the Nottingham Cas-tle Inn.*

Demolished: Left: *Oldknow's House and Chesshyre's House (extreme right), photographed in 1920, at the corner of Ford Street and Friar Gate.* Right: *Corner of St Peter's Churchyard and St Peter's Street, 1882.*

Old Mayor's Parlour in Tenant Street. For its date it was the largest timber-framed town house in England. It was demolished in 1948.

Markeaton Hall, a fine Derby mansion that was demolished in the 1960s.

retains the air of a county market town. The ancient Saxon thoroughfares of the Wardwick and the Cornmarket are still an integral part of the city; narrow Thorntree Lane still snakes down towards the Derwent just as it did when it was a causeway across the marsh, joining Saxon Northworthy with the old British ford.

As the old Morledge Market was closed down in readiness for the new Eagle Centre Market, it was good to see stalls reappear for a time on the Market Place as they did for centuries past. In fact, the very history of the city cries out from almost every street name: in Cheapside where the Saxons held their earliest markets; in Abbey Street where the monks had their barns of grain; in Bold Lane, which was Bolt Lane where the mediæval fletchers made their bolts or arrows; in nearby Jury Street, which was Jewry Street where Derby's Jewish quarter was situated; and in Green Lane where woodland hillside was cleared to form a road between the parishes of St Peter and St Werburgh.

Tenant Street was perhaps near the tenth bridge over Markeaton Brook, or perhaps the name implies tenants *in-capite* — that the townspeople built the bridge with their own money and labour. Sadler Gate is self-explanatory and was the main street leading westward out of the Market Place. Today it

is still one of Derby's most delightful thoroughfares, although the local council could have made a greater effort in attracting the right sort of traders — more in the way of antique shops and less in the way wine bars and amusement arcades. Deadman's Lane was no doubt the burial place of many of the victims of the Black Death which ravaged the town in 1349, 1592-3, 1637 and 1645.

Over the years, Derby has edged ever outwards, swallowing up — but never totally destroying their identity — hamlets and villages which were once outside the boundaries of the old town. Osmaston, Litchurch, Littleover, Mickleover, Shelton Lock, Spondon, Alvaston, Chaddesden and Normanton are just a few of the early settlements which now find themselves under the legislature of Derby City Council.

Normanton is typical of a village which enjoyed one thousand years of independence before becoming part of Derby, but which still retains much of its identity. Founded by the Vikings, its mediæval street, The Portway, linking east and west, still runs through old Normanton today, now as Village Street.

The great urban housing area of Sinfin is a post-World War Two phenomenon. Centuries ago, the Saxons hunted wild fowl

The Old Silk Mill, knocked down in 1920 to make way for Sowter Road and rebuilt nearby.

on the low, damp marshes. Today, Sinfin is the first home for some newly-wed Derby couples as the area grows quickly and now stretches well beyond the city boundary. As new housing goes up on Derby's edges, much of the old inner-city is being pulled down. The so-called Little City disappeared in the 1950s. Until then the area had remained unchanged since the Napoleonic Wars and the street names — Trafalgar, Waterloo and Britannia — bore witness to the origins of the narrow and primitive houses. Even during the reign of the present monarch it was possible to walk down those streets which

had changed not one jot since the time of George III.

Derby's Old West End — which actually owed more to London's East End than to the capital's own plush West End — has disappeared, although some of the old public houses remain to serve the residents of the new housing developments; and in the late 1970s, the tight terraced streets of the Abbey Street-Gerard Street area also fell beneath the bulldozer. With them went a unique social order — a social order which used tiny corner shops and which was judged on the cleanliness of its stone front steps. Gone is

Ashworth the baker where hot bread was extracted from fierce ovens in sight of housewives at the counter; gone, too, is Cordon the greengrocer and Sims the butcher. No longer do Derby men queue for a 'short back and sides' at the barber's shop of Phil Vidofsky — himself brought up in the Little City's Cannon Street. And on a cold, grey day in 1980, the only proof that a large primary school once stood in Gerard Street, was three cricket stumps, rough-painted on what was once a playground wall where successive generations of Derby children laughed and played over a century or more.

New residents took over these areas of inner-Derby, then lying waste awaiting redevelopment. Kestrels, foxes and voles could be seen within sight and sound of Derby's homeward-bound commuter traffic, swooping and scurrying over land where Derby families once sat before roaring coal fires in cramped front rooms. And in the

Derwent, under the thunder of articulated lorries, trout swam under the road bridge, in a river much cleaner than at any time this century. Kingfishers, too, darted amongst the trees near the Old Silk Mill.

In the city itself, shoppers use the Eagle Centre without fear of wet and cold whilst many of the city's older shopping areas are, thankfully, still in use, including the fine old Market Hall, opened in 1864, reconstructed inside in 1938 and in 1991 revamped again. Derby's Council House — seat of local government opened by the then Princess Elizabeth in 1949 — sits on the banks of the Derwent, opposite the Full Street magistrates court and headquarters of the city's county police division. On the site of the old open market sits a splendid new court building. And along the Market Place, where Bonnie Prince Charlie trotted sadly into exile, stands Derby's new Assembly Rooms, criticised by some as dominating the ancient site, but a venue much-

Derby Market Hall pictured in 1985. The hall was later refurbished, allegedly back to something like its Victorian splendour.

favoured by BBC Television and international promoters alike, and a world away from the 1765 Assembly Rooms, the façade of which now stands at Crich Tramway Museum.

Derby residents and visitors can take a trip to the Museum and Art Gallery in the Wardwick and stand in awe of some of the city's historic relics. The *Derby Evening Telegraph* which has recorded local events since 1879, has moved from its green-roofed Northcliffe House — yet another familiar piece of Derby's skyline — and now has a brand-new home on the banks of the Derwent as it moved away from the hot-metal process

The Assembly Rooms in the Market Place, the third building of that name in Derby.

Inside the Eagle Centre in 1985.

and into the age of electronic newspaper production. And since 1971, Derby has had local radio in BBC Radio Derby, based in St Helen's Street, near the site of the town's first monastery in the twelfth century.

Times in Derby, as elsewhere, are uncertain. The economic difficulties that overshadowed the country when the first edition of this book was published in 1980 were followed by the boom years for which we are now paying with a savage recession which threatens to develop into a full-blown slump. As always, there has been good news and bad — the injection of some £37 million of Government City Challenge money and then the decision by the Home Office that the Prison Service would not, after all, be moving its headquarters to Derby.

Yet the Derbeian has always overcome his difficulties and the city's motto, *'Industria, Virtus, et Fortitudo'* (Diligence, Courage, and Strength) has served it well in the past. Since the time that the Roman built his first camps on the high ground near Belper Road and at Little Chester, over nineteen centuries ago, Derby has been destined to play a full part in the story of the British nation. There is no reason to suppose that it will not continue so to do.

Bibliography

Blunt, Canon A.W.F. *The See of Derby* (1929).

Brassington, M. *Roman Derby* (1991).

Cox, J.C. *Three Centuries of Derbyshire Annals* (1907).

Craven, M. *Images of Derby* (1990).

Craven, M. *Derby An Illustrated History* (1988).

Craven M. *The Derby Townhouse* (1987).

Craven, M. *Inns & Taverns of Derby* (1992).

Davison A.W. *Derby, Its Rise and Progress* (1906).

Glover, S. *History of the County of Derby* (1829).

Hutton, W. *History of Derby* (1791).

Jeayes, I.H. *Derbyshire Charters* (1906).

Jewitt, L. *Guide to the Borough of Derby* (1852).

Jones, L.E. *Beauty of English Churches* (1978).

Mallender, M.A. *The Great Church* (1977).

Peters, D. *Darley Abbey* (1974).

Richardson, W.A. *Citizen's Derby* (1949).

Stevens, J. *England's Last Revolution* (1977).

Winter, W.W. *The Winter's Collection of Derby* (1992).

Derbyshire Red Book (1862 to 1915).

Derbyshire Archaeological Society Journal.

Derby Evening Telegraph.

Derby Mercury.

Derby Postman.

Derbyshire Advertiser.

Derby & Chesterfield Reporter.

Origins of Derby and *Mediaeval Derby* (Derby Museum information sheets by Maxwell Craven).

Video

Derby The Story of a City.

Index